DUBLIN CASTLE

in the life of the Irish nation

DUBLIN CASTLE

in the life of the Irish nation

Peter Costello

WOLFHOUND PRESS
Celebrating 25 *Years*

Published in 1999 by
Wolfhound Press Ltd
68 Mountjoy Square
Dublin 1, Ireland

Tel: (353–1) 874 0354
Fax: (353–1) 872 0207

British Library Cataloguing in
Publication Data

A catalogue record for this book is
available from the British Library.

ISBN 0–86327–610–5

10 9 8 7 6 5 4 3 2 1

Design and typesetting by
Joan Roskelly, Bookcraft Ltd, Stroud

Printed by MPG Books Ltd

To the immortal memory of
Sir John Burke, Ulster King
at Arms, and his family, to
whom Irish historians owe
so much

Half title: *The statue of Fortitude (or Mars) by John Van Nost
over one of the arches in the Upper Yard*

Frontispiece: *The southern façade of the Castle, about 1910*

CONTENTS

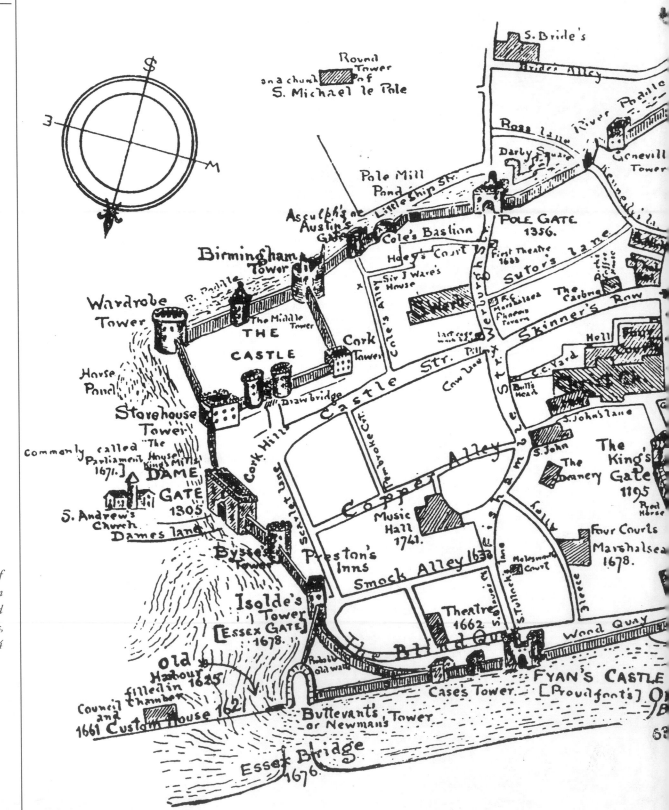

S. Bride's

Round Tower on a church of S. Michael le Pole

Pole Mill Pond

Ross lane

Darby Square

River Paddle

Grenvill Tower

POLE GATE 1356.

Asculph's or Austin's Gate

Little Ship St.

Cole's Bastion

Hoey's Court

First Theatre 1635

Sutor's lane

Birmingham Tower

Sir J. Ware's House

The Carbrie

R. Paddle

The Middle Tower

Skinner's Row

Wardrobe Tower

THE CASTLE

Cork Tower

Cole's Alley

Castle Str.

Hell

C.C. Yard

Horse Pond

Cow Lane

Bull's Head

Drawbridge

S. John's Lane

Storehouse Tower

Cork Hill

Copper Alley

S. John

The King's

Commonly called "The Parliament House" King Mills 1671.]

DAME GATE 1305

Music Hall 1741

Deanery Gate 1195

S. Andrew's Church

Preston's Inns

Smock Alley 1658

Four Courts Marshalsea 1678

Dames lane

Byse's Tower

Theatre 1662

Isolde's Tower [ESSEX GATE] 1678.

Blind Quay

Wood Quay

FYAN'S CASTLE [Proudfoot's]

old

Harbour 1625 filled in

Council chamber and Custom House 162

Probable old wall

Case's Tower

Buttevant's or Newman's Tower

Essex Bridge 1676.

RIGHT: *Map of medieval Dublin created by Leonard R. Strangways, 1904*

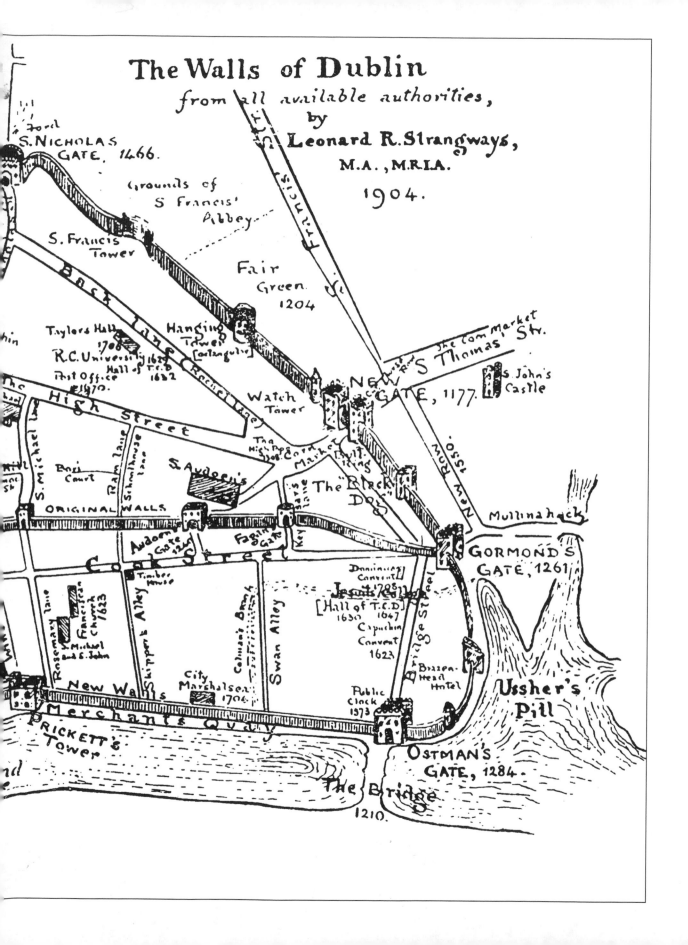

The Walls of Dublin

from all available authorities,
by
Leonard R. Strangways,
M.A., M.R.I.A.
1904.

S. NICHOLAS GATE. 1466.

Ford

Grounds of S Francis' Abbey

S. Francis Tower

Fair Green 1204

Francis St.

Taylors Hall 1706
R.C. University 1625
Hall of T.C.D 1652
Post Office 1970

Back Lane (Rochel Lane)

Hanging Tower [octangular]

Watch Tower

The Cam Market Str.

NEW GATE, 1177.

S. Thomas Str.

S. John's Castle

High Street

S. Michael's Lane

Bull Court

Ram Lane

Schoolhouse Lane

S. Audoen's

The High Cross
Market Butting

Cook Lane

The "Black Dog"

Mullinahack

Key Lane

New Row 1550

ORIGINAL WALLS

Audoen's Gate 1265

Fagan's Gate

GORMOND'S GATE, 1261

Timber House

S. Michael's Alley

Rosemary Lane

S. Francis Church 1623

S. Michael and S. John

Skipper's Alley

Coleman's Bank

Swan Alley

Dominican Convent 1708

Jesuits College
[Hall of T.C.D 1630 1647
Capuchin Convent 1623]

Bridge Street

Brazen Head Hotel

Ussher's Pill

New Walls

City Marshalsea 1706

Public Clock 1973

PRICKETT'S Tower

MERCHANT'S QUAY

OSTMAN'S GATE, 1284.

The Bridge
1210.

LEFT: *Rose Barton,*
Going to the Levée
(1897) – the
historical aspect of
the Castle

PREFACE

In the Victorian heyday of Dublin Castle, the annual social season of the little Viceregal Court which reigned there, opened in February and ended in March, soon after St Patrick's Day, with a Ball. The first event of the season was the Levée, to which several hundred people would be invited by the Viceroy's chief of protocol.

The evocative watercolour by Rose Barton (facing page), entitled 'Going to the Levée,' shows the carriages of the Viceroy's guests moving one by one up Cork Hill and through the Castle Gate into the Upper Yard in February 1897. Only four coaches at a time were allowed in, so the others had to wait in a long queue reaching down Cork Hill and into Dame Street. The elegant ladies and gentleman were the object of scrutiny by the common citizens of Dublin, who commented with ribald freedom on the fine dresses of the women and full figures of the men.

The guests at these events, especially those held a little later under Lord and Lady Aberdeen, were drawn widely from all sections of Irish society, though the opprobrious phrase 'Castle Catholic' was then coming into use by some journalists of the day as a shorthand for this emerging native establishment. Though the Anglican Anglo-Irish gentry were more than well-represented, inevitably many of the guests were from the English staff of the Viceroy, or Lord Lieutenant as he should more properly have been called.

To nationalists of many shades of green, Dublin Castle represented seven hundred years of English rule, and its quaint social life an imposition on the ordinary folk of the Irish nation. Yet the story of Dublin Castle may in reality span more than 4,000 years, in which the centuries of rule by England assume a much less significant part.

In the century since Miss Barton painted her picture, many things have changed in Ireland, and in Dublin Castle. Today the buildings within its confines are used for all kinds of state event, ranging from the inauguration of the President down to judicial tribunals of inquiry, official receptions and exhibitions. Though there is no longer a 'Season' as such, the Castle has become a new kind of institution, in the new, self-confident and prosperous Ireland.

To tell the story of this great Irish fortress, and how this change came about, we have to turn back in time to when there was no Irish nation, to the earliest period of time when the first people arrived in Ireland.

But, to set the scene for this excursion into the far distant past, a short walk around the confines of the present castle – the interior can be left until later – will give the visitor some idea of its external appearance, and of what survives, if only in outline, of the ancient fortress.

RIGHT: *Entrance
gate to Lower
Castle Yard*

THE CASTLE CONFINES

WHAT THE VISITOR CAN SEE TODAY

Turning out of the roaring city centre bustle of Dame Street, we enter the quiet precincts of Dublin Castle through the gate of the Lower Castle Yard in Palace Street. In the old days this was the less formal entrance to the Castle, and today most visitors on foot come this way.

Just before the gate can be seen one of the oldest surviving eighteenth-century houses in the district, the former quarters of the Sick and Indigent Roomkeepers' Society, Dublin's oldest charity, founded in 1790, now lovingly restored by a local artist. Other old houses which stood here have been demolished to create a small open garden, dedicated by the Lord Mayor in 1988, to mark the supposed Millennium of Dublin.

This date actually marked, not the foundation of the city, but the date on which the Irish High King Maolseaghlin exacted tribute from the Norsemen of Dublin, so incorporating them into the Irish community. This was the era '*when Malachy wore the collar of gold / That he won from her proud invader,*' as the poet Thomas Moore recalled. This event, more usually dated to 889, is commemorated also in one of the frescos that decorate the foyer of the City Hall.

In this plot have been placed the classical statutes of the Arts and Sciences that once graced the Exhibition Buildings in Earlsfort Terrace, one of the now-vanished sights of Victorian Dublin.

The City Hall itself, once the Royal Exchange, dominates the skyline. Tucked in beside it is Exchange Place, where the long-infamous Detective Office of the Dublin Metropolitan Police – police work being one of the main tasks of officials at Dublin Castle – was located. This force, incorporated into the Civic Guard in 1925, was one of the world's oldest police forces, having been originally established as far back as 1786 – it was not until 1829 that Sir Robert Peel gave London its organised police.

To the left of the Castle gate a long, narrow street called Dame Lane runs east through the city towards St Andrew's Church, and the site of the ancient Norse assembly place, the Thingmote. This curious thoroughfare, with its high walls, deep shadows, and little shops, recalls the appearance of old Dublin in the time of Jonathan Swift or even earlier.

Through the gate, on the right, is a small shop and café where postcards and souvenirs can be bought. To the left, closing off the east end of the yard, is a modern office block, the home of various government revenue departments; its hideousness is now partially disguised by hanging gardens, the fresh foliage taking away the original concrete rawness. The block is built over what was once one of the guardhouses and the riding school of the Castle.

What we are looking for now is not those parts

ABOVE: *Head of Brian Ború, Emperor of the Irish, on the exterior of the Chapel Royal*

of the Castle erected in recent times, but what can be detected of the earlier periods in its long history. Even today, a walk around the Castle's outer precincts is revealing.

The Lower Castle Yard is dominated by the Chapel Royal. Built on the site of an earlier chapel, its neo-Gothic elegance evokes a medieval atmosphere, even though it dates only from 1807. We need only admire its external quaintness now, as a fuller account of this church will be given later. Heads of Dean Swift and Brian Ború decorate its exterior. The crypt of the chapel is now used as a theatre for various kinds of shows and art events.

Past the apse of the chapel, through a small arch ahead of us, are the old police barracks, quarters still used by the Civic Guards. On the other side of the enclosed yard, where the Carriage Office for Dublin's taxis is now located, a set of steps rises to a small wicket gate giving out into a lane off South Great George's Street. These are still called 'The Informers' Steps', as it was through this gate that the secret agents of the police in the days of British rule crept in with their verbal reports on the criminal and political life of the city (often the same thing in the eyes of the authorities of the time), and collected their pay.

Turning to the right, and walking west, we are now in the bed of the former moat. Running in a hidden channel under our feet is the River Poddle, which formed the ancient moat of Dublin Castle. The Record Tower (once known also as the Wardrobe Tower) looms overhead, with the little door which once gave entrance to the accumulated relics of history in the State Paper Office before its removal to the National Archives. This is thought by some to have been the tower from which Hugh Roe O'Donnell escaped in 1591, and where Robert Emmet was kept a state prisoner in 1803.

12

This tower was the stronghold of the Castle, and may well have a very ancient history. Along here we can see the actual outer limits of the Castle. From this lower point of view, we can better appreciate the position and appearance of the place in the old days, an aspect which cannot be seen from the Upper Castle Yard, where visitors usually arrive today.

In medieval times the blank south wall of the Castle, then forming the outer wall of Dublin city, stood here. Now the façade above us is graced by the elegant windows of the State Apartments, which overlook the Castle Gardens and the stable block. A small octagonal tower stands on the site of one of the castle's original Norman towers.

Going under a little bridge that connects the main reception rooms with the garden, we pass the Bermingham Tower, which takes its name (some say) from the fact that Sir William Bermingham was confined here for treason in 1331 and executed a year later. Or is it perhaps from John de Bermingham, who defeated Edward Bruce at Faughart in 1318? Like the Record Tower, the Bermingham Tower was used as a prison as well as a place to store records.

A striking feature of this long façade today is the bright, almost garish colours in which it has been painted, which strike a hectic note in the muted grey tones of the modern Dublin cityscape.

To the south of this, the countryside in the Middle Ages would have rolled away towards the mountains, which harboured the wild Irish, ready at any moment to make forays against the colonists. Now the city, which slowly developed as more peaceful times came on, has spread out to create a conurbation, the Greater Dublin of today, which runs almost to the border with Wicklow.

Facing this line of walls and towers on our left is the Clock Tower, the new home of the Chester Beatty Oriental Library and Gallery, one of Ireland's great artistic treasure houses, the gift to the Irish nation of mining magnate Sir Alfred Chester Beatty. It contains a world-renowned collection of Chinese and Arab manuscripts, as well as some of the earliest known fragments of the Old Testament, the Gospels and Acts on papyri from Egypt. To international Biblical scholars 'Chester Beatty' has now a ring as familiar as that of the Dead Sea Scrolls. But more impressive to many visitors are the leaves of Arab calligraphy, the Moghul paintings, and Buddhist images.

The gallery overlooks the Castle Garden, which lies on the site of the actual 'Black Pool' of Norse Dublin, where the Poddle spread out to form a large pond to the south of the city wall. Then called 'The Pound', this was once the scene of summer receptions in the days of the Viceroys. It has now been restored, and the lawn is decorated with a mysterious winding decoration intended to represent the eels which once infested the mud of the pool, even down to their bulbous heads. Facing onto the gardens is the old stable block, designed to mimic a miniature castle for toy soldiers.

Behind the new extension to the gallery is Ship Street Barracks – built for real soldiers, but now government offices of various kinds, including the Assay Office of the Goldsmiths Company, where Irish gold and silver has to be hallmarked before it can be sold.

The guilds were introduced into Ireland by the Normans, and they played a leading role in the medieval life of the city. They were granted a Royal Charter in 1637. '*The Company of Goldsmiths of Dublin is the last surviving trade guild,*' remarks Douglas Bennett, the historian of the Irish silver trade, '*and it continues to assay gold, silver and platinum and to this day it upholds the rules and regulations of the original charter, which over the years has been supplemented by various acts of*

LEFT: *Doorway to Chapel Royal, with head of St Peter*

ABOVE: *The Viceroy's seat in the Chapel Royal, with the arms of earlier Viceroys – and St Patrick*

RIGHT: *Hoey's Court, etching by Estella F. Solomons*

parliament [and] government orders to meet changing conditions.' In 1605 the city corporation ruled that each maker must strike his mark on each piece, and among the other early stamps for authentic Dublin silver, along with the Lion and the Harp, should be the Castle.

The Company has been in Dublin Castle itself since 1925, and an assay master and his staff are involved in the daily testing and marking of items whose hallmark is the guarantee of their true worth. For the visitor to Dublin Castle, the Company is a direct link across eight centuries with the founding days of the Anglo-Normans.

Ahead is the back gate of the Castle leading out through Little Ship Street to Werburgh Street – an echo of the 'Men of Bristol' (whose patron saint she was), to whom Henry II chartered the city of Dublin in 1171. Until the erection of the Chapel Royal, the parish church of St Werburgh was used as a chapel by the Viceroys: their reserved place in the gallery can still be seen.

Here in Little Ship Street survives a section of the old city wall added in the thirteenth century – a much-repaired relic of the Normans.

By Austin Gate, just outside the castle, the city wall is pierced on the left by a set of steps which once gave entrance to Hoey's Court, built early in the seventeenth century on the site of what had once been the historian Sir James Ware's residence. In a house on this now-vanished little square the great Jonathan Swift himself was born in 1667.

Above this was Cole's Alley, now Castle Steps. Here in the eighteenth century was a famous resort of billiard players, the Royal Chop House. This warren of old houses has long been swept away, but the refurbished outer wall of the Castle remains. Erected about 1810, as Maurice Craig (the pre-eminent historian of Dublin's fabric) observes, 'the recessed panels emphasise the thickness and impenetrability of the seat of government.' The architect, whoever he was, may also have wanted to suggest something of the original qualities of the medieval fortress.

The wall on the left as we mount the steps

encloses the old cemetery of St Werburgh's Church, in which city notables such as Town Major Sirr, who arrested Lord Edward Fitzgerald and Robert Emmet, lie 'a mouldering in the grave'.

Emerging into Castle Street we find ourselves in an area which also recalls an older Dublin, for this street is as old as the Castle itself. Though now a lonely enough place at certain times, it is one of the most ancient streets of Dublin, and was once the main thoroughfare of the city, where the market place stood. In Scandinavian and medieval times this was where the upper classes of the city lived, whilst the artisans were quartered over towards Fishamble and Winetavern Streets. As early as 1281, this was where the King's Exchange (later used as the Royal Mint) was located. Castle officials lived here. Sir James Ware was born here in 1594. Here, too, was the house of Sir Phelim O'Neill in which the Rising of 1641 was plotted.

It was here in the 1680s that the bankers and booksellers, those two pillars of settled civilisation, were established. To Maurice Craig, again, it was one of the few places in Dublin where something of the medieval atmosphere of Dublin – *'picturesque from a distance, with water-meadows and a still unsullied river flowing past the walls, but at close quarters squalid and constricted'* – might be recaptured by a nocturnal visit.

The old tenements and dark pubs survive on sites here. Until 1813, one of the old wooden-fronted houses still stood on Castle Street, but now it is remarkable for very upmarket new apartments. The south side was long dominated by the La Touche Bank, founded in 1735, which closed in 1870. Newcomens Bank (now the City Rates Office) stood at the eastern end. For a century from 1881 the famous Dublin family of shoemakers, the Barnwells, plied their trade at No. 4. A

ABOVE: *The house in Hoey's Court (now demolished) in which Jonathan Swift was born*

T.H. MASON

RIGHT: *Late medieval timber-framed house which formerly stood in Castle Street*
DUBLIN PENNY JOURNAL

faded notice in their window claimed:

> *Though we use neither Poultice, Plaster or Pill,*
> *We cure sick Soles, no matter how ill.*

The premises have now been restored by the Dublin Civic Trust.

We turn right and, going east, come to the new entrance to the Castle Conference Centre, an elegant bridge arching over the newly-revealed moat; and beyond that to Cork Hill, and the original gate to the

Castle's Upper Yard portrayed in Rose Barton's water-colour. Here, in the grey building to the left, was the office of the Under-Secretary for Ireland, the place from which the whole island of Ireland was once ruled. Here in 1916 the first casualty of the Rising, an unarmed policeman, was shot by the insurgents, and from here in 1940 the air-raid defences of Ireland were directed.

* * *

Having made a circuit of the lines of the ancient Castle, something of its shape and original dimensions will now be clear. Though much changed, like so many of Europe's ancient fortresses, such as the châteaux of France and the German Schlosser, the vestiges of the castle's more primitive origins can still be seen from this viewpoint.

Going through this gate, and under the famous statue of Justice, we come at last into the Upper Castle Yard. In the eighteenth century, in the old days of bribery and corruption, this was called 'The Devil's Half-Acre' from the large numbers of place-seekers who crowded it, hoping for an audience with the Viceroy. To our immediate right is the old Bedford Tower, which once housed the Genealogical Office and under which are buried the old gate towers of the medieval castle. To the east is the cross block (completely rebuilt in the 1960s), and to the west the restored rooms which front St George's Hall, now the scene of various tribunal hearings, and the state-of-the art Castle Conference Centre, which is an essential part of the daily life of the modern Castle.

But the State Apartments are what most visitors wish to see. Today these can be visited only as part of a guided tour, which gathers in the front hall, at the foot of the Battleaxe Staircase.

While waiting for our party to collect, we can leave the visitors, and turn back in the memory of time to the remote prehistoric origins of this fortress overlooking the Liffey.

CHAPTER ONE

THE ANCIENT DÚN OF DUBLIN

In prehistoric times the setting of Dublin Castle was very different from the that which the visitor sees today, though the underlying landscape, the geological foundation of the city's history, persists.

The Setting

The unwalled river Liffey, flowing down freely into the Irish sea from the Wicklow Hills to the south, here widened out into a muddy estuary and flooded over sloblands where Lower Abbey Street and the streets behind Trinity College now stand.

Into the Liffey ran other smaller rivers, one of which was the Poddle. This entered the Liffey around a rise of land on the south bank of the river, known in Gaelic as 'the Hazelwood Ridge'.

Under this ridge lies a reef of rock which provides the real foundation of the citadel in the otherwise peaty soil of the district. This peat, which is mentioned by many earlier writers, now seems to have been largely made up of centuries of organic deposits left behind by successive occupiers of the city.

The Earliest Dubliners

The very name Hazelwood Ridge evokes the well-wooded landscape of prehistory. The Liffey Valley, with its rich resources of fish and game, has been inhabited for

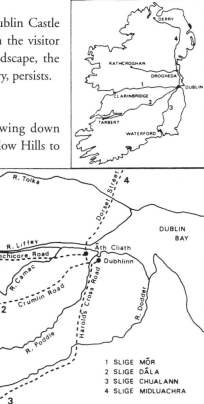

nearly five thousand years. This high ground, surrounded by water on three sides, must have caught the eye of the very earliest settlers as a place which could be easily defended. Though as yet no archaeological evidence has been found, some sort of fort or settlement may well have existed there, if not as early as Neolithic times (circa 2500 BC), perhaps by the end of the Bronze Age and the beginning of the Iron Age (third century BC).

There is a worldwide tendency for sites to remain occupied, and to attract further settlement. Later buildings often lie upon older ones: what is now a fortress may always have been one.

Neolithic and Bronze Ages

The Neolithic and Bronze Age peoples of Ireland are known only from archaeology. They were the predecessors of the Celts, and of a much higher culture. On the evidence of such sites as Newgrange on the Boyne, now known by radio-carbon dating to have been erected about 3200 BC, and to be the oldest surviving stone structure in Western Europe, older even than the Pyramids, they reached a level of skill as mathematicians and architects which was not seen again in Ireland until early medieval times.

LEFT: *The ancient roads of Ireland all converged on the streets of Dublin*

HOWARD B. CLARK

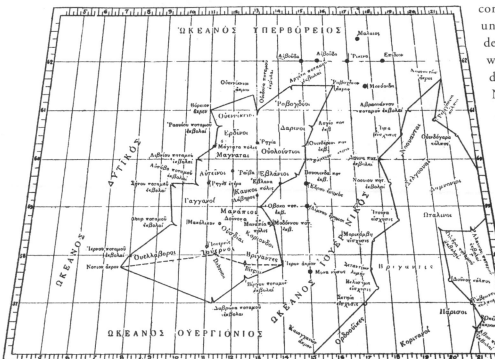

Map labels (Greek): ΩΚΕΑΝΌΣ ΥΠΕΡΒΌΡΕΙΟΣ · ΩΚΕΑΝΌΣ ΔΥΤΙΚΌΣ · ΩΚΕΑΝΌΣ ΙΟΥΕΡΝΙΚΌΝ · ΩΚΕΑΝΌΣ ΟΥΕΡΓΙΌΝΙΟΣ

ABOVE: Long before the Vikings Dublin, under the name Eblana, was known as a trading station by the Greek geographer Ptolemy in the second century AD

Mystery surrounds the prehistory of the Dublin district. Later myths provide a long series of invaders, such as the Fir Bolg and the Milesians, but nothing is really known about who these peoples were. Archaeology provides more material evidence.

At College Green was a series of burial mounds – the Hogges. One excavated in Suffolk Street in the last century disclosed a series of copper axe heads (now in the National Museum collection). These are suggestive of long-established occupation in the immediate area of the Castle.

The Coming of the Celts

The Iron Age is associated with the Celts, who arrived as an invasive warrior class to lord it over the original Irish nation, suppressing their language and culture. The goods of the Iron Age represent a material decline from the wonderful artwork of the Bronze Age, though both cultures existed together for a time. This suggests that the Bronze Age population persisted, changing only slowly. As genetics have shown that the

core population of Europe has remained unchanged for ten thousand years, the descendants of the original Irish may still walk the streets of Dublin along with the descendants of their Celtic, Viking, Norman and English overlords.

The Origins of Dublin

The origins of Dublin city for older antiquarians were wrapped in romance. It was said that Dubhlinn was named after a druidess Dubh who was drowned in the famous pool (linn) below the castle walls. Most archaelogists have doubts about the druids, but all over northern Europe bodies have indeed been found sunk in just such sacrificial pools.

The maritime situation of Dublin must have meant there was a settlement of some sort, but its importance is hard to gauge. Later legend claimed the first invaders of Ireland in myth were the Parthalonians, who settled on the plain between the Liffey and Howth in 2500 AM (Anno Mundi, the Year of Creation) but after three hundred years were wiped out by a plague within a week.

The fact that Eblana, thought by some scholars (though by no means all) to be Dublin, is among the trading places listed by the Greek geographer Ptolemy in his description of the world assembled by AD151, suggests that it was known to merchants from continental Europe, perhaps even to the Phoenicians, those redoubtable navigators from whom it is thought Ptolemy derived much of his information, which reflects the state of settlements about 325 BC.

Certainly this coastline had long been familiar to Roman traders, or even to Roman invaders, who had established some sort of foothold at Drumanagh, a headland to the north of Skerries at Lough Shinny. It was in this area that Eoin MacNeill suggested the Milesians, those last invaders of Ireland, made their first incursion into Ireland, in 3500 AD according to the mythical histories.

In his richly speculative book *Dublin Before the Vikings* (1957), Dr George Little imagined on the basis of surviving place-names that Dublin already existed as a walled-in town in Celtic times: an enchanting fancy which has little appeal to professional archaeologists of today.

But there may well have been a dún – or fortified dwelling – on this height. Recent research suggests, however, that most ringforts in Ireland belong to the early Christian period, despite claims that some had been occupied since the Bronze Age, about 1800 BC. So, by that date at least, there may have been a proto-Dublin Castle.

Given the more recent urban development which has swept away evidence of early life in the Dublin Castle area, evidence is meagre – much has been destroyed since the advent of the Normans.

Early Christian Dublin

Significantly, the great trackways then crossing Ireland, which met at Dublin, spanned the Liffey at the ford, but one continued along the ridge to the approximate site of Dublin Castle today. The Slighe Mhór (coming from the west) and the Slighe Chualann (coming from the north-west) crossed each other at High Street. This point marked one end of the great division of the island into two portions, which tradition recalls as Mogh's Half and Conn's Half circa AD 177. It was also the boundary between two kingdoms, Brega to the north, and Laigin to the south, both of Milesian origin according to MacNeill.

These tracks and two others (from the south-west and the north-east) all seem to have converged on an open space that stood a little to the west of Dublin Castle, on a site where the city cross stood in later centuries, between Christ Church Cathedral and the Castle. This is not surprising, as new roads were as often as not laid down over old ones, just as the streets of modern Dublin run along Viking paths and medieval streets. Anngret Simms has suggested that the original core development of Dublin before 1000 was centred around the junction of Castle Street and Christ Church Place, where it is crossed by Werburgh Street and

Fishamble Street. But these, too, may have lain over the old tracks. Here it seems was the market place of the town, guarded by the dún.

A little to the west was the actual Ford of the Hurdles, which gave the future city one of its names: Baile Átha Cliath, the town of the Hurdle Ford. Whether the hurdles were driven into the river bed as a kind of fence to guide the traveller over the river, or were laid out across the actual mud of the bed to provide a firm foothold – probably the latter – is still undecided.

To the south-east, on the lower ground around what was later St Peter's parish church, there was a sanctuary in Christian times. Possibly this stood on a more ancient pagan site. This is thought to have been called Dubh Linn, Blackpool, from the peat-stained lagoon in the Poddle. Dubhlinn is first mentioned in *The Annals of the Four Masters* under AD 280, when a battle was won there by Fiachara Srabhtine against the men of Leinster. Neither the little village nor the sanctuary could safely have been occupied unless they were protected by a defence work on the height above.

There is another possibility that the enclosure of Dubh Linn was actually the one on the eminence, around what is now Christ Church Cathedral. From the seventh century there are records of the bishops of Dublin. Later lists add the names of the abbots of the local monasteries. The scattering of ancient dedications suggests that these churches were connected with early settlements. In early Christian times the city area had seven ecclesiastical sites, two of them major ones.

Yet some archaeologists still feel that the area was only lightly settled with no real significance as road junction, trading post or population centre. If the total population of the island of Ireland was only half a million, numbers must indeed have been thin on the ground around Dublin.

I imagine this early Dublin then must have been very like Ankober, the ancient capital of Shoa in medieval Ethiopia, where the thatched huts and the primitive little churches of the people lay strung out along a ridge below the king's fort on the flattened summit of the overlooking hill.

Myths and Legends

St Patrick's conversion of Dublin was traditionally dated to AD 448. There was then a local king and a clan to baptise at the well where St Patrick's Cathedral now stands. There are occasional references in the Gaelic annals to Áth Cliath, but as much of the historical literature actually written in Leinster has been lost, the original settlement may once have had a more important place in local chronicles.

'Isolde's Chapel', and one of the towers on the city walls at Essex Quay was called 'Isolde's Tower'. Curiously Tristan seems to have been an historical figure of the sixth century AD, at a time when Cornwall was a vassal kingdom of the Irish – it will be recalled that the tragedy of the couple has its origins in a tribute exacted by an Irish king from the Cornish King Mark, also known as Cunomorius.

A mile and a half north of Fowey in Cornwall is

ABOVE: *St Patrick lighting the Paschal fire, painting by Vincenzo Valdre on the ceiling of St Patrick's Hall*

AN DÚCHAS THE HERITAGE SERVICE

The history of St Patrick and the times he lived in are obscure. But his work, and that of Auxilius and Sechnaill, left profound changes, including the founding of many churches. It is likely that here, as elsewhere in Europe, Christian churches were erected within older pagan precincts.

There is also the curious Arthurian connection hinted at in the romance of Tristan and Isolde, with which James Joyce makes great play in *Finnegans Wake*. Chapelizod to the west of the city is said to have been

an ancient standing stone, on which is carved the inscription HIC IACIT DRUSTANS CUNOMORI FILIUS – Here lies Drustans [that is Tristan] son of Cunomorius [Cynfawr]. Given the associated place-names in Dublin, perhaps Isolde's father was king of that city some time about 539 AD (the date of the battle of Camlann at which Arthur was killed). Or so it seems medieval Dubliners believed. But such an ancient king at Dublin, however attractive to civic pride, seems a moot point to many archaeologists and historians.

Viking Dublin

Whatever may be the reality hidden in the early myths and legends, the actual history of Dublin begins in 838 or 841 with the arrival in the river of the Norsemen, who with 'three score and five ships landed at Dubhlinn of Áth Cliath' to plunder the district. Their pirate lair is now thought to have been further upstream at Islandbridge or Kilmainham. The nineteenth-century discovery of what seems to have been a large Viking cemetery at Islandbridge, which included a great quantity of household items, has led J. Graham-Campbell to suggest that the original Viking boatstead was close to this site, upstream from Dublin proper. This would have left it undisturbed by the tidal rise and fall in the river.

This may well have been the longphoirt mentioned in early records, and not the Blackpool behind the Castle. It could be that their post was where the Royal Hospital is today, a site protected on three sides by the Cammock and the Liffey.

The archaeological record has to be merged with the historical record such as it is. The first Norse arrivals were reinforced by others in 852–3, led by Olav the White. He was joined by Ivar the Boneless, who had led many raids on England, and succeeded Olav as king of Dublin in 871.

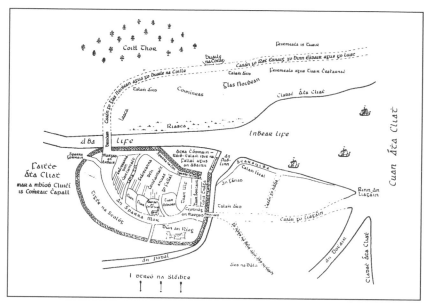

ABOVE: *Map of Dublin as it appeared to the ancient Irish*

SEOSAMH Ó NÉILL, GAOTH ADTUAIDH, 1940

Yet Stanihurst (writing in the 1570s) records that when the first Vikings arrived they took Dublin by stratagem. Having noticed that birds were nesting in the roofs of the houses, they caught some of them and attached wildfire to them, and the birds flying back to their nests set the houses alight. Whatever the truth about this, the implication is that there was some sort of defended settlement at Dublin in Celtic times. The houses found by archaeologists are built not in the Norse manner but in the Irish style, suggesting that the builders were more local than was once thought. The latest data speaks of 'Anglo-Saxon'-style houses – even more non-Norse.

LEFT: *The houses of Viking Dublin*

DRAWING COURTESY DR PATRICK WALLACE, NATIONAL MUSEUM OF IRELAND

The first Vikings were Finn Gaill, or Fair Strangers, followed a little later by Dubh Gaill, or Dark Strangers, the distinction made by Gaelic historians between the Norsemen from Sweden and Norway, and the Danes. The Finn Gaill erected a fixed fort or camp which is seen as the true beginning of Dublin.

This second wave in 849 are said to have slain everyone who defended the Dún of Dublin and to have pillaged the places of all jewels, goods and hangings. The Vikings, having been driven out by the Irish in 902, returned in 917. This time they fortified, or re-fortified, the present site on the ridge to the east of Christ Church Cathedral. Whether Celtic trading post, actual town or adjunct to an ecclesiastical sanctuary, this site must have been defended in some way.

Excavations in 1961 under the Upper Castle Yard (when the cross block that stood along the line of the old medieval east wall was demolished) revealed a layer of Viking occupation, the first indication of the extraordinary discoveries to be made later on in other areas of the old city, and showed that by 1100 the early earthen defences had been replaced by a solid city wall.

But none of the modern excavations around the Castle has produced material as early as the ninth century. Patrick Wallace, the chief excavator of Viking Dublin, argues that the Viking city was in fact founded in the tenth century by a further wave of Scandinavian settlers from Britain, among whom were some Anglo-Saxons and some native Irish.

Around the core of the first Viking settlement the town expanded westward between 1000 and 1100, with further suburban settlement outside the ring of the city walls. Over the next century the town became an important centre in the Viking world and eventually a little kingdom was carved out, reaching north to Skerries and south to Wicklow (itself a Viking name) and west to Lucan. This colony, whose contacts reached from Russia to the New World, was ruled by the descendants of Ivar down to 1042.

The Celtic tribes made occasional efforts to dislodge the better-armed invaders. The last real attempt was made at the battle of Islandbridge, when Niall Black-Knee, the High King at Tara, was killed in 919.

LEFT: Brian Ború, rallying his soldiers before the battle at Clontarf in 1014

But, as happened elsewhere in Europe, such as in northern France, the Norsemen assimilated to themselves some aspects of the local culture around them. During the tenth century Dublin was taken from time to time by Irish kings, but they were happy to levy a tax on the prosperous traders rather than destroy the place. Towns had never been a part of the way of life of the insular Celts, although on the Continent, under the influence of Greece and Rome, towns did emerge.

22

The Viking fort may have resembled that which can still be see at Birka, the great trading centre on an island in Lake Malar in Sweden, There an earthen wall encloses an area which runs to the edge of a steep cliff. The actual settlement stood below this and was eventually enclosed with a wall. Some of the anchorages lay beside the town, others outside it. The Viking forts and towns appear to have been influenced by those they had seen in the Slavic lands to the east. These were described by the Arab traveller Al-Bekri as being laid out in a round or square form on open ground, with earth from a ditch being used to make the walls which were reinforced with planks and posts 'in the manner of ramparts'. The Viking trading town at Dublin followed a similar pattern.

The Last Days of the Vikings

The Vikings intermarried with the Gaelic kings and took sides in their disputes. They took part in a revolt against Brian Ború ('the Emperor of the Irish') in 999, which was put down. Another revolt, or family quarrel, broke out fourteen years later. Then at the Battle of Clontarf in 1014, the mixed army of Leinstermen, Dubliners and Vikings was defeated by Brian's army, though Brian himself was killed. The Norse king of Dublin followed the course of the battle on the northern bank of the Liffey from the walls of his fortress on the south bank.

This was the last moment when Ireland might have created a strong central monarchy, such as was emerging across Europe. But after Brian's death the kings

BELOW: *The Battle of Clontarf as seen by a Victorian Irish artist*

23

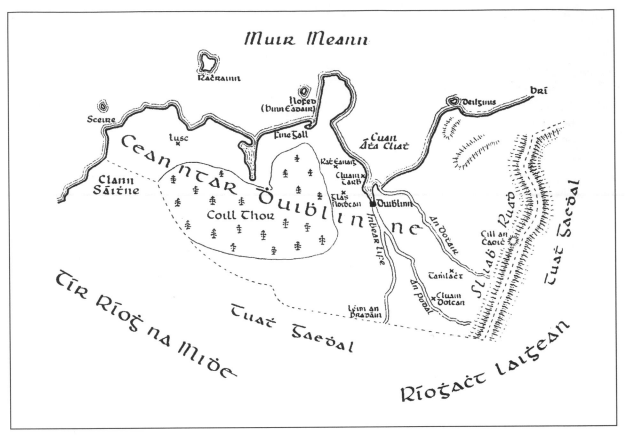

LEFT: *Map of the Norse Kingdom of Dublin as it appeared to the surrounding Irish and the invading Normans*

SEOSAMH Ó NÉILL, *GAOTH ADTUAIDH*, 1940

fell back into their old quarrelling ways. The Viking kingdom, however, under Sigrist Silken Beard, survived. By now Dublin had become a Christian city, and it was under Sigrist (who issued the first coins in Ireland) that the original Christ Church Cathedral was erected, modelled on the great wooden churches of Norway. Though the city's first bishop was a Gael, he was sent to England for consecration.

The town had now achieved its essential shape, dominated by the Norse fortress on the hill, with streets running down to moorings on the Liffey banks. To the east, on an open green area, was the Thingmote, the assembly place of the Norsemen. Here had been the sanctuary of the Scandinavian gods, now turned into the church of St Andrew.

Sigrist Silken Beard died in 1036. The power of the Vikings waned, and they came under the domination of the Kings of Leinster, whose realm ran across the Irish Sea to Man. This remained the situation until the reign of Dermot II of Leinster in the mid twelfth century.

In the endemic feuds of the period, the city sided with the High King against Dermot, who was driven into exile. But Dermot secured the patronage of the Plantagenet King of England, Henry II. After a brief foray in 1166, he returned with a small army of Norman knights and their followers in 1169. Further Normans followed. On 21 September 1170, St Matthew's Day, these allies took Dublin by stratagem.

With the arrival of the Normans, a new era began for Dublin and its fortress.

GIRALDUS CAMBRENSIS

ON THE STORMING OF THE CITY OF DUBLIN, AD 1170

Dermot, however, knowing that almost all Ireland had been summoned by the citizens of Dublin to aid in the defence, and that every road leading to the city ran through wooded defiles held by the enemy, remembered the disaster that befell his father, and avoiding the forest country led his army along the mountain ridges by Glendalough, and brought it safely to the city walls. For he held the inhabitants of Dublin in deeper detestation than any other of his enemies in Ireland; and not without reason, since they had murdered his father in the great hall of one of his chief men where he was accustomed to sit in public to administer justice, and had added insult to injury by burying a dog with the body. Envoys, however, were sent from the city, and preliminaries of peace were entered into through the special mediation of Laurence, of blessed memory, then archbishop of the see of Dublin.

But in the mean time on one side of the city Reginald, on the other a certain Milo de Cogan, a valiant officer, with a following of the younger soldiery thirsting for fight and plunder, carried the walls with a rush and descended boldly into the city, making much slaughter among the people. The greater number of these, however, led by Hasculf, got on board their galleys and boats with their more valuable effects and sailed off to the Northern Islands. On the same day two great miracles happened in the city. A crucifix which the citizens tried hard to carry away with them to the isles became immovable; and a penny which was twice offered before the same, twice leapt back.

(Milo de Cogan was left by the earl as governor of Dublin. Roderic of Connaught, in retaliation for an irruption by Dermot and his allies beyond the borders of Leinster into the territory of his old enemy O'Ruarc, king of Meath, after in vain warning Dermot, put to death the son of the latter whom he held as a hostage.)

BELOW: *The marriage of Aoife and Strongbow, an epic painting by Daniel Maclise*
NATIONAL GALLERY OF IRELAND

CHAPTER TWO

THE NORMAN CASTLE

To secure his alliance with his foreign allies, Dermot married his daughter Aoife (Eva) to Richard de Clare, Earl of Pembroke, known as Strongbow, the leader of the Norman invaders. When Dermot died, Strongbow made himself King of Leinster, quite contrary to traditional Gaelic custom.

He was then attacked in Dublin by the Gaelic High King and the Viking Earl of Dublin. The Earl was captured and executed, but the Normans were nearly overwhelmed by a siege of the city. They made a last desperate foray, and taking the Gaelic army by surprise from the rear, routed it. Though smaller in numbers, the Normans again carried the day against the Gaels.

Norman Dublin now seemed secure. But the significance of the arrival of these knights, themselves of Viking descent, who were spreading across Europe and changing the political landscape from England to Sicily, escaped the petty Gaelic kings, intent as they had always been on their own local quarrels.

Against the superior arms and armour of the Normans, the Gaelic soldiers, poorly equipped and fitfully led, were no real match. The medieval war machine (the contemporary equivalent of modern rapid armoured divisions) defeated the prehistoric tribalism of the natives. The possibility now emerged that the Normans in Ireland would carve out for themselves a new kingdom which would rival and threaten England.

The Irish themselves had invaded Strathclyde, South Wales and Cornwall: it was only to be expected that there would be some incursions from England into Ireland. But what was not foreseen was the long-term consequences, when what had been an adventure by a small group of Norman barons was changed into an extension of the English king's authority, backed by a Papal blessing. After the murder in 1170 of Thomas á Becket, the martyred Archbishop of Canterbury, Henry II needed to make favour with Rome once more. How better to do so than by setting the quarrelsome Irish to rights?

In 1171 Henry II, anxious that Strongbow was creating an important base in Ireland, came over to exact homage from his subjects in Ireland. He arrived in Dublin on 11 November, and set up a palace 'roofed with wattles after the fashion of the country'. This is thought by some scholars to have been on Hoggen Green (now College Green), but may well have been on the site of the Norse king's own palace, where the present castle now stands.

ABOVE: *Henry II, enthroned in Dublin, to receive the homage of the Irish kings*

DRAWING BY SUSAN HAYES, AFTER MS 700, NATIONAL LIBRARY OF IRELAND

This scene was later painted, in fanciful terms, by Vincenzo Valdre on the ceiling of St Patrick's Hall.

Strongbow was forced to surrender the city and kingdom of Dublin to the Crown. The city was granted by charter to the men of Bristol, and became essentially the main base for the slow English conquest of Ireland. It would remain the centre of English rule until 16 January 1922 – 761 years in all.

The Norse were removed to Ostmantown on the north bank of the river, around Stoneybatter, and slowly became submerged into the population of the wider city. The native Irish were forced out into Irishtown, to the south of the river Dodder. But here they remained a distinctive clan until recent times, specialising in boat building and fishing. Though local government emerged in the city of Dublin itself, the Castle remained the symbol of the Royal presence – and power – in Ireland. That power was exerted through the primitive form of civil service that then existed – something unknown in the Gaelic kingdoms. The more evolved form of this civil service still runs the governance of Ireland to this day – perhaps the most lasting, most permanent aspect of Ireland's Norman heritage.

RIGHT: *Norman soldiers in chain mail armour*

When the Normans arrived in Ireland they had fortified their captured territories with motte-and-bailey castles. These consisted of a mound with a wooden fort on the summit, at the foot of which was an enclosure surrounded by a stockade. They were very suitable for frontier conditions, but in Dublin this was not enough. Something more was needed there. This is not to imply that there was no fort already there from Viking times, for we know that there was; but merely that it too was made of wood and earth, after the fashion of Viking forts across northern Europe.

What the Normans first erected is not known. We know that by 1194 there was a bridge and a ditch, and inside that a tower. But this would have been something like a motte-and-bailey, such as the one at Dinant in Normandy, shown on the nearly contemporary Bayeux embroidery. However, this tower may have been the original of what is now the Record Tower.

On 30 August 1204 in the sixth year of his reign (just when the English crown lost Normandy), King John issued a mandate to Meiler FitzHenry (a bastard offspring of Henry II), his justiciar in Ireland.

'You have intimated to us that you have no place about you where our treasure can be laid up; and in as much for that purpose as well as for many other a fortalice may be necessary for us at Dublin, we give you mandate to have a castle made there in a suitable place where you shall see best so as to curb and, if need be, to defend the city, making it as strong as you can with good ditches and strong walls. And you shall first make a tower

whereat a later time the castle and bailey and other requirements may be suitably made, provided we shall give you mandate for that. At present, you may take for this use 300 marks from G. FitzRobert, in which he stands indebted to us.'

Here at the very beginning of its history we find the English king trying to maintain Dublin Castle on the cheap – a continuing feature throughout the history of the castle.

The plan of this citadel covered roughly the present area of the Upper Castle Yard. Meiler may well have only improved the tower on the commanding height of the Upper Yard (where the Record Tower is today – though Harold Leask was of the opinion that the first keep was the Powder Tower).

Though the writ for the building of the Castle was issued in 1205, it took many years to complete, suggesting that after this initial fortification another castle, to a larger design was contemplated, the work

28

being largely undertaken first by de Gray, Bishop of Norwich and Viceroy of Ireland, and by his successor Henry of London, archbishop of Dublin and again Viceroy. He is said to have completed it circa 1215, but work went on to a much later date. Up to 1228, payments were being authorised to workmen fitting up the towers of the Castle. Much is still uncertain about these early years of the Castle. The western wall was rebuilt, a city fosse or ditch was dug along the south side, and the old Viking walls of the city were repaired.

The role of bishops in this moment of Irish history may seem odd, but from the king's point of view they were most useful as they would have no heirs to set up in lands of their own. One of Henry's first acts in landing in Ireland had been to call a synod of the Irish bishops at Cashel to confirm his rights under the Papal Bull Laudabiliter. This, too, was an indication of the importance of the hierarchy in imposing the royal will on the country.

Dublin Castle, however, was no ordinary fortress. It was at the leading edge of castle design, importing its defensive ideas from France. The influence of such contemporary erections such as the famous Château Gaillard on Dublin Castle have been detected, with the use of a keep incorporated into the curtain walls, and the open court and drawbridge. It also resembles such German castles as the Jagdschloss at Grunau bei Neuburg. Lessons had also been learned from the building of castles in the Kingdom of Jerusalem, which the Crusaders had carved out in the Holy Land. It may in fact have been the first castle in these islands built from foundations up in the latest manner. This gives it an important European status.

The new buildings in Dublin were being constructed of stone, which was all imported from quarries scattered around the islands. The plan of the Castle followed what would become a familiar plan of corner towers and curtain walls. The most significant of these is the Record Tower, on the south-eastern corner. This was originally the Wardrobe Tower, where robes and regalia were stored. It was used to hold prisoners, often the hostages which the English took from the native chiefs. On the south wall was the Bermingham

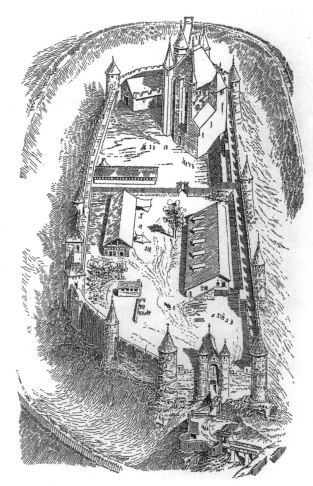

RIGHT: *A bird's eye view of the château of Arques, the new style of European castle on which Dublin castle was partly modeled*

(or Kitchen) Tower, which was used as a prison as well as for keeping the records now so essential to government. On the north-west corner was a tower which collapsed on 1 May 1622, which was called Cork Tower after Richard Boyle, Earl of Cork, who rebuilt it at his own cost in 1624. On the northern flank was a barbican gate leading out into Castle Street and the city proper.

Very little of the fabric of this original thirteenth-century castle survives today, and what does is hidden out of sight or buried underground. In the Undercroft in the Lower Yard, however, can be seen the base of a tower, a postern door and a water-gate, all of which were excavated by archaeologists in 1986-7. The Record Tower, though it has been revamped, retains much of its medieval appearance. And under the Bedford Tower are the remains of one of the old gate towers, which was

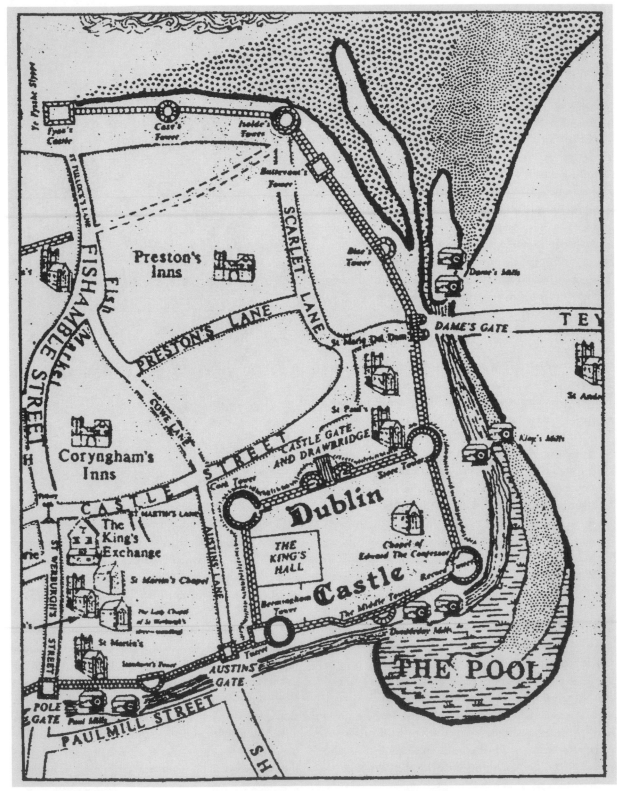

RIGHT: *Map of the medieval castle and city of Dublin*
FRIENDS OF MEDIEVAL DUBLIN

rebuilt in 1617 to replace the original.

Around the whole Castle was a moat called the Castle gripe. There were two small sallyports, one into Sheep (now Ship) Street. There was also a chapel (the chaplain of which got an annual salary of 50 marks), a mint, a mill (called the King's Mill), the Exchequer, a kitchen and buttery, and a hall. (Some of these are mentioned as early as 1224.) The Constable of the Castle was paid £20 per annum. The first Viceroy to get a salary was Geoffroi de Marisco to whom Henry III granted £580.

1855. By then it had become a byword for violence and debauchery, and the prim citizens of nineteenth-century Dublin were not as tolerant as their medieval ancestors, since Donnybrook had by then become a respectable suburb.

In 1207 Dublin was granted a new charter by King John, but the security of the citizens still left much to be desired. On Easter Monday in 1209, while they were enjoying themselves at Cullenswood (in modern Ranelagh), they were attacked and many of them killed.

BELOW: *Interior of a château which approximates to the style of medieval Dublin Castle*

This work was to be carried out at the expense of the citizens of Dublin. As compensation they were granted a royal charter for an annual fair. This was the famous Donnybrook Fair, held for eight days after the Feast of the Invention of the True Cross, in August. It would last until the days of Queen Victoria, being abolished only by the purchase of the Royal Patent in

The Black Easter Monday massacre at Cullenswood – a massacre which was commemorated in the city down to 1690 – made the colonists uneasy for their future. The new castle, it was hoped, would overawe the wild O'Byrnes and O'Tooles who held the hill country in nearby Wicklow.

Between 1212–13 and 1220 Henry of London

completed the Castle (according to Camden's *Britannia*, though Ware's *Annals* suggests that only the main walls were completed by 1228, and that the towers were added at later dates). In any case, such large-scale fortifications, which would also have included city walls, gates and towers, took many years to complete.

This was not the end of the construction, for both the city and the Castle were considerably enlarged by the Viceroys sent to Ireland by the early Plantagenets. In 1243, Henry III, a pious lover of art and literature but a weak king, had the New Hall added, making it the most elaborate building in Dublin to date, with running water and 'with glazed windows after the manner of the Hall at Canterbury' – window glass being the epitome of civilised advance. Windows were added to the chapel, dedicated to Edward the Confessor, in which two chaplains were now provided to say mass every Saturday with fifteen wax candles (though on other days they were restricted to four).

As was often to be the case, work was begun by the king in 1243, only to be suspended the following year. But the hall was eventually completed. This must have been (aside from the great abbeys) the most impressive building in Ireland. It had marble columns, a raised dais surmounted by a fresco of Henry III and his queen Eleanor of Provence, surrounded by their barons (largely his opponents), a large rose window and piped running water. This came from a tank on the roof and the Castle was the first building in Ireland to enjoy this amenity of new technology.

Though the existence of these buildings is known from the records, their exact location and layout is not. Though there is nothing medieval about what we can see today, the Plantagenets intended the castle to be a stylish principal building in the new capital of their colony.

Dublin Castle (like those at Limerick and Kilkenny) was a keepless castle.

The layout of the medieval Castle is known from a seventeenth-century plan made by Thomas Phillips (now in the National Library of Ireland), and an inventory of 1585 which gives details of the various towers, and the loops and windows in them. But, despite the fragmentary documentary evidence, there is much that is not known. Only further excavations, to be made as the opportunities arise, will clear away the mist of uncertainty.

CHAPTER THREE

THE ENGLISH STRONGHOLD

Dublin Castle now represented the centre of English power in Ireland, the heart of the Pale where the English writ ran. As such it had great symbolic value, which would have to be maintained. During the years 1267 to 1268 alone, some £342 was spent on the fortifications of the Castle. Though the occasional parliaments met in the Great Hall, its primary use was for administration and as a dungeon for state prisoners.

In 1307 the Irish Knights Templar were imprisoned in the Castle by Sir John Wogan, at the time of their general suppression throughout Europe for supposed heresy, though in Ireland, where they had been established since the 1190s, there was nothing to compare with the persecutions in France. After the trials,

KING ART MAC MURRAGH AND THE EARL OF GLOUCESTER, A.D. 1399.
FROM MS. IN BRITISH MUSEUM.

LEFT: *King Art MacMurragh and the Earl of Gloucester, an encounter between two very different cultures in 1399*

SIR JOHN GILBERT, FACSIMILES OF THE NATIONAL MANUSCRIPTS OF IRELAND, 1878 which were held in Dublin between January and June 1310, their preceptories were seized by the Crown and given to the Knights Hospitaller in 1313.

In May 1315 Ireland was invaded from Scotland by Edward Bruce, the brother of Robert Bruce who had defeated the English at Bannockburn the year before. He was seeking a new field for his energies in Ireland. The hope was that the Gaelic kingdoms of Ireland and Scotland could be united against their common encroaching enemy. Bruce was crowned King of Ireland at Dundalk in May 1316. He broke the power of the English in Ireland but, after a campaign that devastated the island, he was himself defeated at the battle of Faughart, near Dundalk, and killed by John de Bermingham on 14 October 1318.

He had laid siege to Dublin briefly in 1317, during which part of the city was burned before he was defeated. The city defences were not in good order and emergency measures had to be taken, even the bridge over the Liffey being taken down. The mayor attempted to clear away the suburbs by burning down part of them, but the fire spread and much damage was done to the city itself. Recent excavations in Castle Street unearthed a ditch which is thought to have been part of these emergency defences. The parliament, which was due to meet in Dublin, was called instead to Kilmainham by Edward II. The Scottish army, which had been camped at Castleknock, moved off, and Dublin was safe.

If Dublin was left relatively unscathed, this invasion had important consequences for Ireland's history as it weakened the Norman colony and the Dublin government. The progress of conquest paused, but the old Gaelic order did not revive. The Norman settlers were now intermarrying with the Gaels, and a new nation, the historic Irish nation, was in the making.

In 1320 the Great Hall was repaired, which involved taking down and re-erecting the wall. A decade later, the windows of the Great Hall were filled with stained glass.

Dublin was remote from mainstream Europe, but not from the ravages of disease, as the arrival of the Black Death, or bubonic plague, showed in 1349. There

RIGHT: *The famous Irish gallowglasses, used in the wars with the English*

were numerous deaths, and the plague in Ireland – as elsewhere in Europe – weakened the authority of the government. It had come from China, by way of the Crimea, destroying '*a third of the world*' and giving many Europeans the belief that '*this is the end of the world*'.

In Ireland a friar named Brother John Clyn, left alone among the dying, continued to keep a record of events, fearing '*that things which should be remembered perish with time and vanish from the memory of those who come after us*'. The whole island was, it seemed to him, '*placed within the grasp of the Evil One*'. Around Dublin alone, some 14,000 are said to have died. This was a national disaster which eclipsed even the Great Famine of 1847 yet, as Brother John feared, it has, it seems, vanished from the memory of those who came after.

* * *

The structure of the Castle was rebuilt (it seems) by Lionel, Duke of Clarence, who was appointed King's Lieutenant by Edward III in 1361. The Castle itself was actually in the care of a Clerk. In 1372 there is a reference to John Moore, Clerk of the castle works; and in 1381 there was an inquiry into the defects of the building. A resident Constable was responsible for the safety of the Castle, as at the Tower of London and Caernarvon Castle; but in the seventeenth century his duties were absorbed by the office of the Viceroy, and the office became a sinecure.

Ireland became a matter of royal concern with two visits to Ireland by Richard I towards the end of his reign, in 1394 and 1399. He received the submission of the Irish kings, but this was not of any real consequence, for the writ of English law ran only within the Pale, approximately the county of Dublin and parts of Louth, Meath and Kildare. Richard returned to England to face defeat. The problems of their own country kept the English from ruling effectively in Ireland.

A drawing survives from the fourteenth century which shows the Court of Exchequer meeting in Dublin Castle, around the table with the chequered cover from which the court took its name. The royal funds were kept in Dublin Castle (as indicated by the mandate to build it) and were controlled by the treasurer and two Chamberlains of the Exchequer, all three of whom had to be present with their separate keys to the locks on the coffer in order for any payments to be made. This must have proved frustrating for the King's creditors in Ireland from time to time!

In 1411 the Bermingham Tower was added to

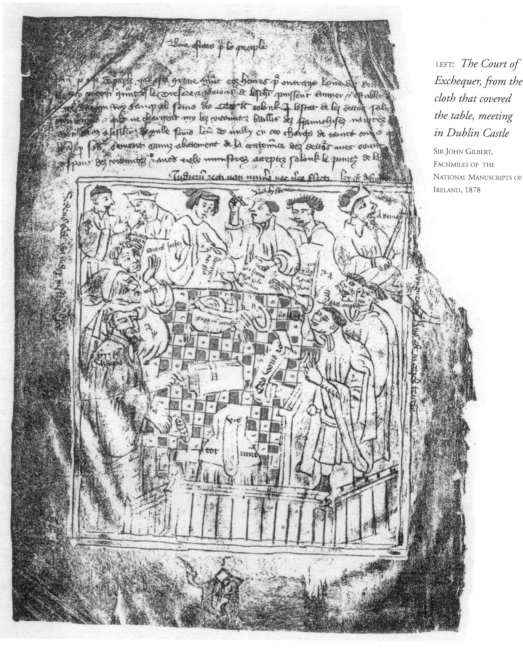

LEFT: *The Court of Exchequer, from the cloth that covered the table, meeting in Dublin Castle*

SIR JOHN GILBERT, FACSIMILES OF THE NATIONAL MANUSCRIPTS OF IRELAND, 1878

Dublin Castle. A scattering of records from this time give some indication of its role in official life. In 1422 John Conyngham was appointed Keeper of the King's Palace within the Castle of Dublin, with an annual fee of 100 shillings. Yet by 1430 the hall, towers and other buildings were reported to be in a ruinous condition, and the state records held there were being damaged by

English armour (NEAR RIGHT) *was superior to that worn by the native Irish soldiers* (FAR RIGHT)

rain. The sum of 20 marks a year was allowed for repairs. Yet in 1435 the Constable of the Castle was still reporting to the Council in London that the frost and bad weather '*have these last three years so impaired and hurt the walls of the Castles of Dublin and Wicklow which will entail right great and notable summs unless they be sooner repaired and mended*'.

Though in 1459 brass coins were made in the mint set up in Dublin Castle, in 1462 there was yet another report that '*the Castle ... of Dublin ... wherein the courts are kept, is ruinous and likely to fall*'.

It was ordered that the leads of the aisles of the hall be sold to make and repair the hall, all of which sounds very like cheeseparing and making do. However, an allowance was made of 80 shillings a year for repairs of the courts at Dublin Castle.

The Castle played its own role in the Wars of the Roses, when Richard of York escaped there after the Battle of Ludlow, only to be later killed at the Battle of Wakefield.

In 1463 Edward IV appointed an Irishman as Lord Deputy. This was Thomas, Earl of Desmond, one of those Norman families with extended Gaelic family connections. Yet he lasted for only five years before being removed and virtually murdered by the Crown, and his great rival Thomas FitzGerald took his place, bringing into prominence and power the great Geraldine family.

The Parliaments still met in the Castle from time to time. Here, too, were the royal stores and magazines, and the Courts of Justice. Yet the actual administration had weakened, and the offices were largely filled by nominees of the great Anglo-Irish families, who were more concerned with securing their own power than in furthering the King's claims in Ireland. In 1478 the Earl of Kildare was to have been replaced as deputy by Henry, Lord Grey. Kildare refused to resign. He was supported by the Constable of the Castle, James Keating (a cleric who was also Prior of Kilmainham).

To prevent Grey from entering the Castle and assuming his office, Keating tore down the drawbridge from Castle Street. Keating was ordered by a parliament held later that year to repair the bridge at his own expense. But the majesty of England was not to be thwarted. Keating was later deprived of his two offices and ended his life in poverty.

The medieval Dublin which had developed since 1200 was very different from the old Norse city. Instead of the low thatched cottages which excavations have revealed, there were now two- or three-storey houses in the English style, with wooden frames and plastered walls. The city had drains of a kind and running water. It had become even more prosperous from trade, not only with England and Europe but within Ireland as well. The customs of dress and manners which were

common in Dublin became the style for the Irish lords and chiefs. Though the wild Irish were still unconquered, cultural change was drawing them further into medieval life, just as the Normans were being drawn into the old Irish culture.

Now, with the ascent of the Tudors in 1485, after the Battle of Bosworth finally brought the Wars of the Roses to a conclusion, the final stage of the conquest begun by Strongbow could be completed.

This would involve a renewed role for Dublin Castle.

ABOVE: *A fourteenth century interior in a richly endowed castle*

LEFT: *In contrast to the small houses of Viking times, houses of medieval Dublin were large and comfortable*

37

ABOVE: *Guns
altered forever the
task of besieging a
city*
RAPHAEL HOLINSHED,
THE HISTORIE OF
IRELANDE, 1577

CHAPTER FOUR

THE VICEROY'S PALACE

Under Henry VII, the first of the Tudors, Dublin was the main scene of the strange drama of that claimant to the English throne, Lambert Simnel. He was recognised by the Earl of Kildare and the citizens, lodged in Dublin Castle, and crowned in the cathedral as Edward VI on 24 May 1478. He was supposed to be one of the Princes in the Tower, the rightful Yorkist heirs, who had escaped the clutches of the usurper Richard III. (The princes had probably in fact been murdered by agents of King Henry soon after Bosworth, though it was alleged by Tudor apologists such as St Thomas More that they had been murdered by Richard.)

Simnel was carried from the cathedral to the Castle on the shoulders of the great D'Arcy of Platten, the tallest man in Ireland. This scene, too, is shown on the frescos that today decorate the City Hall, just outside Dublin Castle. His supporters were soon defeated, and he was said to have been sent to work in the royal kitchens where he invented Simnel cake, which used to be eaten at Eastertide. But King Henry had less patience with Perkin Warbeck, another claimant in the 1490s: he had his head chopped off.

This era was perhaps more significantly marked in 1487 by the first use of guns in Ireland, by the soldiers of Aodh Ruadh Ó Domhnaill, when Brian Ó Ruairc was shot at the seizing of Castlecar in Leitrim. The advent of guns was to make castles in the old medieval style obsolete. As with the Normans' chainmail, this technology would have great social consequences. It meant that the government had to store large amounts of dangerous gunpowder in the Castle, which led to accidents. But it also meant that sieges would become a thing of the past,

the historical initiative passing to mobile armies.

Ireland, and Dublin, remained unsettled and violent. In 1493 the Mayor of Dublin, John Sargent, was imprisoned in the Castle after a riot in Oxmantown in which several people were killed. But the introduction of Poyning's Law by Henry in 1494 'restored order to Ireland', at least from the English point of view.

The Statutes of Drogheda provided that no Irish parliament could be summoned except under the Great Seal of England, and that the acts of any parliament in Ireland would not be valid unless submitted to the Privy Council in London, and that all English acts passed prior to 1494 should have force in Ireland. (Poyning's Law was not repealed until 1782, when the Irish Parliament under Grattan asserted its independence.) Having repelled Perkin Warbeck's invasion, Poyning left Ireland in 1495.

In 1500 Dublin was besieged by the Earl of Kildare. The Geraldines were the most powerful family in Ireland, and the government worked for their suppression. The accession in 1509 of Henry VIII marked the commencement of a new period. In 1525 Con O'Neill and Hugh Roe O'Donnell came to Dublin to try to settle their disputes with the Lord Deputy, the Earl of Kildare and the Council, but failed.

Of more serious consequence was the rebellion in the summer of 1534 by Thomas Fitzgerald, Lord Offaly ('Silken Thomas') — so called from the gorgeous silk jackets of his horsemen. This was described by one historian as 'the most serious revolt against English authority of which the capital has ever been the scene', though it had little military significance elsewhere. The

Geraldines, under Garrett Mór, who had been Lord Deputy, had been Yorkists. His son Garrett Óg was called to London by Henry VIII to face a charge of treason, leaving his young son Thomas to govern the country in his absence. Believing his father to have been killed in London, Thomas arrived in anger at a meeting of the Council in St Mary's Abbey, and remonstrated against the king. Urged on by his poet, he threw his

sword of office on the table and departed an avowed rebel, '*an flung awaie like a bedlam, being garded with his brutish drove of brainsicke rebels*'.

Thomas tried to take Dublin Castle by storm. His first attack was a frontal one on the main gate. But the citizens of Dublin had already warned the Constable of the Castle and supplied him with food. The siege was easily withstood and, with news that the King's army was on its way, a counter-attack was made and many of Thomas's followers were captured. He now attacked the south gate of the Castle in Ship Street, but was driven off by the castle guns. Thomas now switched the assault to the Thomas Street gate but, by the ruse of pretending that help had arrived, the Castle garrison finally routed

him. Though he escaped, the rebellion collapsed, he was forced to surrender, and he and his five uncles were executed in London. Thus ended the one really serious siege of Dublin Castle.

In 1534 Dublin was shaken by an earthquake, an omen of other upheavals to come. In May 1535 George Browne, the archbishop of Dublin, conformed to the Thirty-Nine Articles of the Anglican confession. The Reformation that had been sweeping over Europe since 1517 had reached Dublin. As churches were changed and the property of the monasteries seized, the ancient Catholic relics, among them St Patrick's staff, were taken from Christ Church Cathedral and burned.

Ireland beyond the Pale remained largely Catholic, and on the defensive. The defeat of O'Neill was followed in 1541 by Henry VIII declaring himself King, rather than mere Lord, of Ireland. This Kingdom of Ireland was to last until the Act of Union in 1800. '*Henry set up in Ireland,*' wrote Edmund Curtis, '*all the style and trappings of Monarchy, a Royal great seal, courts of law, a Privy Council, and so on, but in fact it was a government controlled from England, in which national representation found little place, and exercised through English-born viceroys.*' For these Viceroys Dublin Castle was the centre of Ireland. Now it remained to match the claim of that authority from Dublin Castle with rule on the ground.

To this time belongs the foundation of what is now the oldest office of State in Ireland, the post of Chief Herald, established in 1552. The officials were the Ulster King-at-Arms, with two heralds, Cork and Dublin; and two pursuivants, Athlone and St Patrick. The whole purpose of the office was grandly feudal, a fine full flowering of the medieval outlook. They were installed until 1903 in the Record Tower, amid their parchments, hatchments and chronicles.

Though the Viceroys had been resident after the Reformation at the old monastery in Kilmainham for a time, much of their life was still centred in the Castle. But the Castle with its prisons was not an ideal location for the court – after the latter were removed, the Castle fell into disrepair.

The Reformation gathered pace, so much so that

heralding an even more remote event, the Great Irish Famine. But of greater consequence was the Papal bull denouncing Elizabeth as a heretic and absolving her Catholic subjects from loyalty to her. The English anxiety about this palpable attack on the state was the making of many Irish martyrs. Though the numbers are uncertain, the great mass died either under Elizabeth or under the Commonwealth. The circumstances were

BELOW: *Sir Henry Sidney rides out from Dublin Castle to overawe the Irish*

JOHN DERRICKE, THE IMAGE OF IRELAND, 1581

many Protestants sought refuge in Dublin under the brief reign of Catholic Mary from 1553 to 1558. She was followed by Elizabeth, even more determined to subdue the troublesome Irish than her father had been.

In 1560 Dublin Castle was fitted up as the chief residence of the chief governor of Ireland. The wars against the O'Neills are the chief feature of the Castle's history at this time, but other events were also significant. The importation in 1566 of seven hundred English bibles to be sold in the city heralded the religious nature of the wars to come. In 1565, when the walls of Wood Quay and Merchant's Quay were repaired, potatoes were introduced into Ireland from Santa Fé by John Hawkins – though some now think this was the sweet potato –

always cruel, but then, from the viewpoint of the day, this was war.

Between 1565 and 1578 Sir Henry Sidney, the Queen's man in Ireland, rebuilt and repaired the Castle – turning it from '*a ruinous, foule, filthie and greatly decayed*' fortress into what Holinshed called a '*verie fair house for the Lord deputie or the chiefe governor to reside and dwell in*'. The new apartments were, however, on the site of the old. During this period in 1571 the first printing in Gaelic was undertaken there by Nicholas Walshe. Sidney was an exacting ruler; in 1577 he detained protesters over taxes in the Castle.

In 1578 the walls of the Castle ditch were repaired by the city, an indication of the anxiety with which the citizens viewed their safety. The following year (1579) the records of Ireland were arranged in the Bermingham Tower – this is perhaps the beginning of the State Paper Office, now part of the National Archives and removed to Bishop Street.

For once we know something about what the Castle looked like at this period, for a woodcut of it was included among the illustrations of Irish life and character included in John Derricke's *Image of Ireland*, published in 1581. This shows Sir Henry Sidney and his retinue riding out of Dublin Castle through the arch of the main gate, above which the heads of executed Irish rebels are impaled on spikes. A poetic tag of the day, quoted by Derricke above this print, warns:

> These trunckless heddes doe playnly show each rebelles fatall end,
> And what a haynous thing it is the quene for to offend.

In recent excavations, archaeologists have recovered from rubbish pits male skulls which were clearly beheaded and spiked.

The picture shows clearly the barbicans of the gate-house, the Castle walls and ditch, and beyond them the continuation of the city wall, with Christ Church looming up over the house tops. Outside the city walls the houses of the newly-developing suburbs can be seen in the Liberties.

In 1582 the Law Courts, which had been held in the Castle since Norman times, were moved across the river to the former Dominican Abbey, now the site of the Four Courts. This was also outside the city walls, but part of the growing settlement that was expanding on the north bank of the Liffey.

But not all legal matters left the castle. In 1583 a trial by combat was held in the castle yard before the Lords Justice. It was between two of the O'Connors. Tiege MacGilpatrick O'Connor won the bout and cut off the head of his opponent, presenting it to their lordships. Oddly enough this form of trial, which astonished many later writers by its medieval barbarity, survived in English law until 1818, when it was last resorted to by Abraham Thornton. In some states of the USA it is still law, it seems.

In 1585 the Parliament in Dublin passed regulations against priests entering the kingdom. This was a dark and dismal time in Ireland, when martyrs were made easily. These martyrdoms had begun, not under Henry or Edward, but in 1572 under Elizabeth and continued under James I.

One of the most conspicuous of these was the Archbishop of Cashel, Dermot O'Hurley, who was arrested when he came to Dublin, and was imprisoned in the Castle, '*that dark and fetid prison*' as a contemporary historian called it. He was questioned and tortured, and was finally executed on 20 June 1584. Other martyrs who were detained and tortured, and died in the Castle, included Mrs Margaret Bell. She was arrested at the instance of her son Walter who had been elected Mayor of Dublin. He had her drawn through the streets on a wooden hurdle, as she could no longer walk. She was held a prisoner in the Castle for the remainder of her life. If she had agreed to take the Oath of Supremacy she could have been released. But she refused and lingered on in the Castle where she died in about 1584 at the age of 69. Even the great Countess of Desmond and her children were detained there, though she survived.

In 1587 Hugh Roe ('Red Hugh') O'Donnell, then aged only eighteen, was captured by treachery in his father's territory in Donegal by agents of the Viceroy: he was tempted aboard a ship at Rathmullen on Lough Swilly to sample its cargo of wine. He was brought to Dublin, where he was imprisoned in the Castle. In one of the great romantic incidents in the history of the fortress, he escaped not once but twice, in December 1590 and again in December 1591, eventually making his way south into the Wicklow Hills.

He was created Lord of Tyrconnell in May 1592 (his father having resigned the title), submitting to the Lord Deputy at Dundalk in August. However, he and Hugh O'Neill maintained their resistance as long as they could, achieving a noted victory at the Yellow Ford in August 1598. But the old Gaelic order was collapsing. After he and O'Neill were defeated at the battle of Kinsale in 1601, O'Donnell went into exile in Spain, dying at Simancas in the following year.

He is thought to have been held in the Record Tower, where a room used to be shown to visitors as his cell, though the account of his escape says he escaped into the city first. The escape of O'Donnell features in a film made by Walt Disney *The Fighting Prince of Donegal* (1965), adapted from a novel by an American writer, which seems to be the only time the ancient fortress – as distinct from the modern castle – has been shown on the screen.

The Elizabethan conquest of Ireland, paralleled by the contemporary colonial adventures in the New World, was a bloody business. It united the Gaelic clans with the Old English who remained Catholic, but through a series of native rebellions the rule of England spread. The advent of the Spanish Armada caused concern, but the survivors cast up on the west coast were hunted down and killed, those harbouring them being tortured and executed. Dublin with its Castle was now the chief power in the land.

Dublin, of course, was changing too. In 1596 a shipment of 144 barrels of gunpowder exploded while being unloaded at Wood Quay. They had been intended for the magazine at Dublin Castle. The blast destroyed between forty and fifty houses, killing some three hundred Dubliners, and damaging several of the city's churches. If the explosion had occurred in the Castle itself, nothing would have been left.

On John Speed's Dublin map of 1610 the gaping hole made in the fabric of the city by the blast can clearly be seen, still largely contained within the medieval city walls. Speed's was the first map of Dublin, showing the city as it was known in Elizabethan and Jacobite times, and the Castle was among the most significant buildings on it, as befitted its place in history.

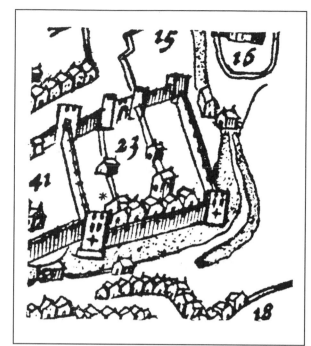

LEFT: *Dublin Castle as shown on John Speed's map of Dublin in 1610*

THE ESCAPES OF HUGH ROE O'DONNELL FROM DUBLIN CASTLE, 1590–91

It became known immediately throughout the whole city and to the Lord Deputy and the Council especially that they had come after this manner, and that Aodh Ó Domhnaill. was in their custody. They were glad of his coming, and it was not at all through love of him, and they summoned him to them without delay that he might be face to face with them, and they proceeded to converse with him and ask information of him, and in a special way they observed and searched into his natural qualities. In the end, however, they ordered him to be put in a strong stone castle where the noble descendants of the sons of Milesius were in chain and captivity expecting death and doom, together with some of the nobles of the Fingallians who had come to the island long before and had entered into amity and friendship with the Irish against the English, who came last from the country of the Saxons to take the island from both of them. It was their solace and satisfaction day and night in the close prison where they were, to be lamenting over the insufferable hardships and relating the great cruelty which was

43

inflicted on them both English and Irish, and hearing of the lying judgments pronounced and the wrongs and wicked deeds done against the high-born noble descendants of the sons of Milesius and of the Fingallians in general …

He was always meditating and searching how to find a way of escape. This was no easy thing for him, for he was put each night into a well-secured apartment in the castle for security until the morning of the next day came. That castle was situated thus. There was a broad deep trench full of water all round it and a solid bridge of boards over it opposite the door of the castle, and a grim-visaged party of the English outside and inside the gate to guard it, so that no one should pass them, in or out without permission from the foreign warders. However, there is no watch of which advantage may not be taken at last. One time, just at the end of winter, when Aodh was with, a number of his companions, in the very beginning of the night, before they were put into the well-secured cells in which they used to be every night, they succeeded in bringing a very long rope to the window in front of them, and they let themselves down by the ropes until they alighted on the bridge outside the door of the castle. There was a very strong iron ring on the door to draw it out to oneself when desirable. They put a bar of solid wood a fist thick through the ring, so that no one should come in haste out of the castle to pursue them … As for the guards, they did not perceive the escape for some time; and when they perceived that the youths had got off, they went at once to the gate of the castle as fast as they could, for they thought they would catch them instantly. When they came to the gate, it was impossible for them to open it or to draw the gate in; so they set to call to them the people who happened to be in the houses opposite the gate on the other side of the street. After coming at their call, these took out the bar which was through the ring and they raised up the gate for the people of the castle. A great crowd of the city people went in pursuit of the youths who had escaped from them. This was not easy, for these were outside the walls of the town before they were noticed, as the gates of the royal city were wide open then. They went towards them and leaped over fences and enclosures and walls outside

the town until they stopped at the slope of the mountain opposite them due south. This mountain is long and very wide; it was the boundary between the Irish of the province of Leinster and the English of Dublin. Its roads and ways were numerous, but fear did not allow them to go by the usual roads. Moreover, they did not delay on their way till they crossed Sliav Rua before that morning, though fatigued by the journey and travelling all the night. As they were tired and weary, they went into a dense wood which happened to be on their way, and they remained in it till early dawn. They prepared to go on after that, for they did not think it safe to remain in the wood, owing to the fear and great dread of being sought after and looked for by their enemies …

As it was certain to Feilim and to his relatives that anyone else might find him, they resolved to take him themselves and bring him back to the city to the Council. That was done. When he came to Dublin the Council were delighted thereat, and made little or no account of all the hostages and pledges who escaped from them, and they were thankful for the good fortune which restored him to them again. Though great their cruelty and enmity to him the first time, they were greater the second time on account of his escape from them, and iron gyves were put on him as tight as they could be, and they put him in the same prison and they watched and guarded him the best way they could.

He was in this way in the same prison throughout the year to the following January to Twelfth Night in the year 1592. When it seemed to the Son of the Virgin full time that he should escape, he and some of his companions took advantage of the guards in the very beginning of the night before they were taken to the refectory, and they took off their fetters. They went after that to the privy, having a long rope, and they let themselves down by means of the rope through the privy till they came to the deep trench which was around the castle. After that they climbed to the opposite bank, till they were on the edge of the trench at the other side. The hostages who escaped with Aodh were Enri and Art, the two sons of Seán, son of Conn Bacach, son of Conn, son of Enri, son of Eóghan. There was a certain faithful servant who visited them in the castle as a horseboy, to whom they imparted their secret, so that he met them face to face when they wanted him to be their guide. They went off after that through the crowded streets, in front of the castle, without being known or overheard by any one, for they were not noticed except like every one else of the city people, as they did not stop to converse with or visit any one whatever in the houses of the city at that time, for it was the beginning of the night exactly and the gates of the city were not yet closed. They went out through the city in that manner. They leaped over the roughness and impediment of the thick rampart and of the strong, huge palisade which was outside the city, until they came to the slopes of Sliav Rua, where Aodh had come before, the first time he escaped. The darkness of the night and the hurry of the flight separated him who was the oldest of the party from them. This was Enri Ó Néill. Aodh was the youngest of the nobles. They were not pleased at the separation. They went away, however, their attendant leading the way. The night came on with a drizzle and a violent downpour of rain and slippery slime of snow, so that it was not easy for the high-born nobles to walk on account of the inclement weather and the want of clothing, for they had no outer garments, having left them in the privy through which they had come.

LEFT: *The meeting of Hugh O'Neill and the Earl of Essex in September 1599, the climax of the Elizabethan wars in Ireland*

From the *Book of Lughaidh ó Clérigh*

45

BELOW: *The first map of Dublin, by John Speed, showing the city in 1610*

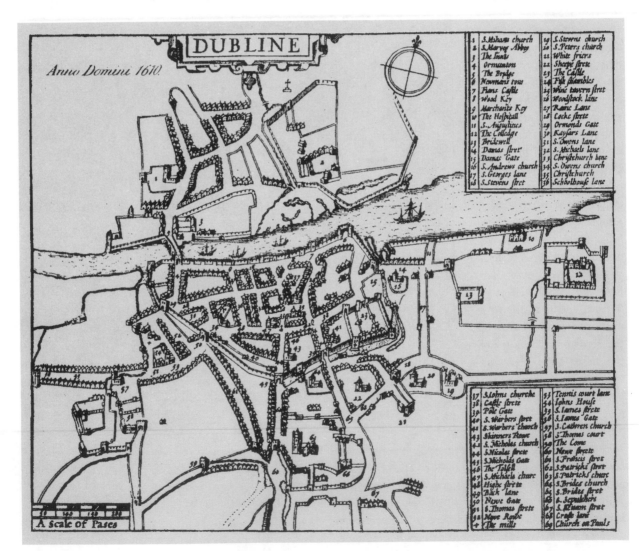

CHAPTER FIVE

THE CASTLE BETWEEN KING AND PARLIAMENT

The ascent of the severely Protestant James I to the throne in March 1603 brought with it little amelioration of English policy in Ireland. The king was proclaimed in Dublin on 5 April. That month, Catholic clergy repossessed churches in some rural towns, but this movement was quickly quashed. In 1605 several of the Aldermen and principal citizens of Dublin were brought before the Castle Chamber and fined for nonconformity to the Church of Ireland.

Then, in the mysterious way of the seventeenth century, a letter was found, in the same council chamber of the castle, charging the Earls of Tyrone and Tyrconnell with treason. They escaped from Ireland to safety abroad in September 1607. This symbolic event became known as 'The Flight of the Earls', from which many nationalists later dated the final doom of Gaelic Ireland. Their lands were confiscated, their followers killed and evicted, and new Protestant settlers were planted in the western counties of Ulster. What Elizabeth had begun, James would continue.

The Castle was once again at the centre of a renewed attempt to conquer Ireland once and for all, but the Old English who remained Catholic would now be in alliance with the Gaelic families. In 1607 the imprisonment and escape of Richard Nugent, Lord Devlin, was also an indication that oppression would continue, even if the Castle could still not hold all its prisoners.

Parliament assembled in Dublin after a lapse of thirteen years, and the Castle once again returned to prominence. From 1606 there survives a rough plan, on which are scribbled suggested changes that might be made to the structure, none of which were in the event

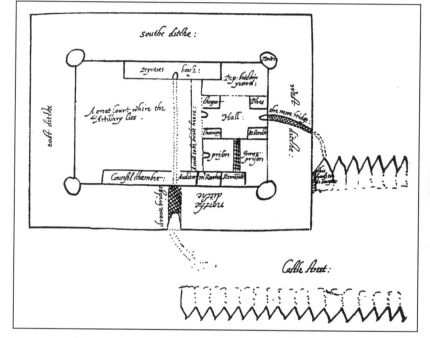

ever carried out. After entering the Castle across the bridge shown in Derricke's drawing, to the left was the Council Chamber, and on the right a set of small reception rooms. Directly across the yard ('A great Court where the Artillery lies'), was the Deputy's House, where the State Apartments now are. To the right of this was the kitchen. On the west wall of the Castle was the Great Hall, to which it was proposed a new bridge should be made, and beside this two large prisons.

In 1617 the gatehouse leading out of the castle into the city was rebuilt. The fabric of the castle was elsewhere in decay. In 1624 a proposal was made to tear down the tower at the north-west corner – only for it to

BELOW: *Watson's plan of the Castle in 1606*

collapse a few days later.

In 1633 Thomas Wentworth was appointed Lord Deputy of Ireland (Lord Lieutenant, 1640). Though he had once opposed King Charles I, he was now a supporter of royal absolutism, and in Ireland he began to apply what he calls in his letters a 'thorough' policy. One success was the suppression of piracy on the Irish coast. He married in Dublin Castle, and it was Wentworth who began the social entertaining there that would be such a large feature of the future life of the Castle.

Created Earl of Strafford in 1640, he advocated the use of Irish troops against the Scots, and this was the beginning of his downfall. When the Long Parliament assembled in 1640 its first work was to investigate Strafford and, largely at the behest of his enemies in Ireland, to impeach him. The king could not protect him and he was executed in May 1641 on Tower Hill. All this was a mere preliminary to more turmoil.

On his death the Castle remained in the hands of the Lords Justice, acting for the Long Parliament, while the Duke of Ormonde, his actual successor as Viceroy, was in command of the Royalist forces at Kilkenny.

* * *

ABOVE: *Cromwell on his ruthless course through Ireland; one of his sons was born in Dublin Castle*

48

Hence I went to the Castle, wherein my Lord Deputy resides, within which are both the Houses of Parliament, whereof I took a view: much less and meaner than ours. The Lords' House is now furnished with about sixty or seventy armours for horse, which are my Lord deputy's: this is a room of no great state nor receipt ... Here in this castle we saw the council-chamber, wherein stands a very long table, furnished with stools at both sides and ends. Here sometimes sit in council about 60 or 64 privy councillors. here we saw the hall, a very plain room, and with the dining-room, wherein is placed the cloth of state over my Lord Deputy's head, when he is at meat. Beyond this is the chamber of presence, a room indeed of state ... We went to Sir Thomas Rotheram (who is a privy-councillor), who used us respectively, and accompanied me to the Castle, and showed me the courts of justice, which are conveniently framed and contrived, and these very capacious.

Sir William Brereton, Travels in the United Provinces, England, Scotland and Ireland, ed. Edward Hawkins (London, 1844)

* * *

On 23 October 1641, the advent of the English Civil War was marked in Dublin by the failed attempt of Sir Phelim O'Neill to surprise Dublin Castle and seize the capital. This plot failed because of treachery, but the rising went ahead. Up to 12,000 Protestants were killed during the next six months of war, a slaughter that left a bitter memory in Ulster.

In the following year (1642) the English Civil War began. Like the Wars of the Roses this was to have echoes in Ireland. During the Commonwealth Dublin Castle continued to play its role as a centre of administration. Further attempts

were made from time to time to seize it, as, for example, by a corporal and seventeen desperadoes in April 1646.

Though the Duke of Ormonde repulsed the army of the Catholic Confederacy from Kilkenny, he had to surrender to the Commonwealth a little later in 1647. Colonel Jones, governor under Cromwell, repaired the walls. Ormonde later attempted to take the city but was defeated by Michael Jones at the Battle of Rathmines in 1649.

Cromwell himself arrived in Dublin in 1649 and remained until October, during which he 'subdued Ireland', killing some 4,000 people at Drogheda alone. As townsmen these unfortunates might better be thought of as English too, but the massacre at Drogheda was later incorporated into the mythology of Irish nationalism. The native Irish were given the famous choice of 'To Hell or to Connaught,' and their leaders were uprooted to estates west of the Shannon. During his time in Ireland Cromwell lived in Dublin Castle, where one of his sons was born.

Under the Commonwealth, Ireland's first taste of republican rule, the persecution of the Catholic Church was pursued with a ferocity even greater than that under

BELOW: *Plan of the Castle in 1673*

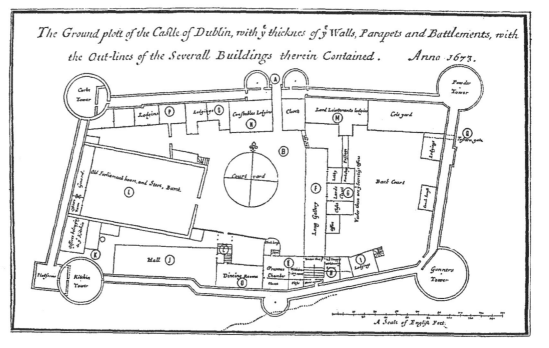

Elizabeth. In four years, more died than in the whole of her reign. For the Irish the curse of Cromwell was a terrible passage in history.

In 1652 Ireton replaced Cromwell as deputy, and he in turn was followed by the energetic Henry Cromwell, popular with the English settlers, who kept great state in the Castle.

With the death of Oliver Cromwell in 1658, the Irish parliament resolved that the government of Ireland

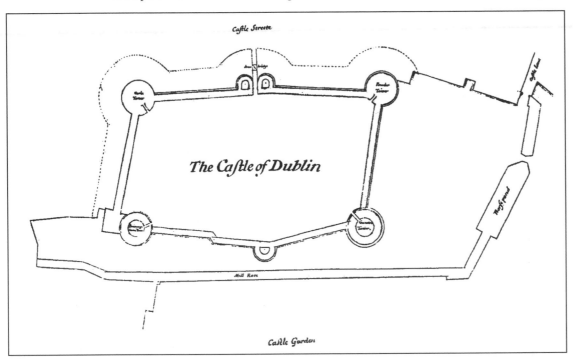

The Castle of Dublin

ABOVE: *Thomas Phillips' plan of the Castle in 1685*

should be through parliament and not by any one man. Ironically this first move towards parliamentary representative democracy came under a repressive régime which excluded Catholics. However, it was already clear that the days of Richard Cromwell, who had inherited his father's title of Lord Protector but not his character, were numbered, and a clique of officers favouring the restoration of Charles II seized Dublin Castle in 1659. Such was the king's gratitude to the city that one of his first acts in 1660 was to present it with a new chain of office for the Mayor.

The executions of Catholic priests ceased, and between the Restoration (1660) and the advent of

Queen Anne (1714) no-one was executed, although some confessors of the Catholic faith died in prison, and one was killed near Buncrana.

In 1663 that curious adventurer Colonel Thomas Blood (c.1628–80) was caught in a plot to seize Dublin Castle and capture the Lord Lieutenant. For his military services to Parliament he had been awarded estates in Ireland, but he lost these at the Restoration. Later he would attempt to kidnap and hang the Duke of Ormonde (1670) and steal the Crown Jewels of England from the Tower of London (1671), for which he was mysteriously pardoned by Charles II, leading some to suspect that he was a royal bastard.

The great Duke of Ormonde became Lord Lieutenant from 1662 to 1669, and again from 1677 to 1685, and it is with him that the modern history of Dublin and of Dublin Castle can be said to begin. Given the great symbolic value of the Castle to the city and to the country, Ormonde was forced to restore it in some style. From an inventory taken in 1679 we learn that he provided it with Turkey work chairs in the dining room, gilt leather hangings in his dressing room, tapestry, crimson velvet chairs and silver furniture in the drawing room. All of this was lost in a fire that ruined the state apartments a few years later.

Much of the structure of Dublin Castle, which by now was a cramped and higgledy-piggledy collection of post-medieval buildings, apart from the actual viceregal quarters, was destroyed by a fire in 1671.

But at the time little was done to repair this loss.

This fire marked the end of the old medieval

castle. The buildings we see today date largely from the seventeenth century and after, so that the plans prepared for them by William Robinson mark the beginning of the the modern era in the history of the Castle. The old structure was pulled down in part by 1685, but the plans were not yet complete for its replacement. Whatever work had been begun was delayed further when Robinson fled to England when the Catholic Tyrconnel became Viceroy in 1687, though work was continued in part by William Molyneaux.

In 1678 Catholics had been forbidden even to enter Dublin Castle, a consequence of the anti-Catholic mania in England. Peter Talbot, the Catholic Archbishop, was arrested and imprisoned in the dungeons during the Popish Plot instigated by Titus Oates. He died there in 1680. Now Tyrconnell took over the Castle chapel for Catholic use. Fire once more swept the Viceregal quarters in the Castle on 7 April 1684. The acting Lord Deputy, Lord Arran, acted with dispatch when he discovered the fire, blowing up parts of the fabric to prevent the fire from spreading to the Record Tower or, worse still, the Powder Tower. '*I find,*' he reported, '*that the king has lost nothing except six barrels of powder and the worst castle in the worst position in Christendom, for his Majesty's goods are saved from the fire and for the value of the ground it stood upon, and the land belonging to it, his Majesty may have a noble palace built, and I believe there are a hundred projectors at work already about framing proposals.*'

In the event, plans for rebuilding were drawn up by William Robinson from a concept by Molyneaux. Shortly after the fire Thomas Phillips was sent to Dublin to survey the situation. '*The Castle or Chief Seat of the Government being all in Rubbish by the late Fire, and when in Perfection not capable of securing his Majesties Stores of War without great hazard of being destroyed by fire, it being so pestered up with houses and other offices.*'

He suggested that the Vice-Regal Court and the fortress should be separated. He wanted a great star-shaped citadel along the bank of the Liffey near Irishtown. But, as was to be so often the case in the future, this expensive plan was not followed. Instead the Castle was restored, presumably to the designs of Sir William Robinson, the Surveyor General of the day. Robinson had already been responsible for the Royal Hospital at Kilmainham in 1680, and would later design Marsh's Library (1702) and the Hall of the South Dublin Union (1703). A drawing now in the British Museum associated with this rebuilding, with same use of arcades as at Kilmainham, is thought to be from his office.

The fire of 1684 gave Ormonde the opportunity to remove himself to the far more pleasant King's House at Chapelizod, where his successors were to remain until the creation of the Viceregal Lodge in Phoenix Park in 1801. The Park was itself a seventeenth-century creation, for it had been enclosed and stocked with game by Ormonde.

In 1685 James II came to the throne. Suspected of Catholic sympathies, he was distrusted, and soon a plot to impose his daughter Mary and her husband William of Orange on the throne came to a head in 1688.

By October 1689 the work on the new apartments seems to have been completed, as it is recorded '*that the new buildings in the Castle of Dublin was finished and the Lord deputy removed from Chapelizod, for that house was disturbed with spirits that they could not rest*'. But the Viceroy was about to be plagued by more than mischievous poltergeists.

In 1688 the new castle was said to be finished and Tyrconnell moved in. But a few months later William and Mary landed in England to depose the king, and the Williamite wars began. Tyrconnell attempted to refortify the castle, but luckily it was not besieged during the struggle for the throne.

ABOVE: *The statue of William III in College Green, the focus of many Loyalist demonstrations in the nineteenth century*

CHAPTER SIX

THE CASTLE AND THE PROTESTANT NATION

On 13 February 1689 James II landed in Ireland; and in March 1689 Dublin Castle received the King, who entered the city with far less pomp and circumstance than his Lords Deputy had done. He came on horseback, with his two natural sons riding beside him, and Richard Talbot, the Earl of Tyrconnell, carrying the sword of state. He was very courteous to the citizens as he passed, but 'it was said he wept as he rode into the Castle'.

The campaign, which had European dimensions, was to be settled on Irish soil. The Siege of Derry followed in December 1689, and the Battle of the Boyne in July 1690.

On 7 May 1689 James II called an assembly in Dublin Castle, which later came to be called 'The Patriot Parliament'. This, as Edmund Curtis observes in the language of the new Ireland, 'was the last legislative assembly of the older Irish race up to 1922, and the last in which the Roman Catholic faith was represented'. During this stay the Catholic Mass was again celebrated in the Castle – for the first time since the Reformation, and the last time until 1944.

The hectic scenes in Dublin during the brief visit of James II, and his flight after the Battle of the Boyne on 12 July 1690, when he spent a night in the Castle before fleeing to exile in France, followed by the arrival of William of Orange, marked a final settlement of the city.

The Irish army was defeated at 'Aughrim's great disaster' and though the treaty of Limerick was supposed to secure the position of Catholics in law, it did not do so. Tyrconnell died of poison. Thousands of Irish soldiers went abroad, 'the Wild Geese' in flight from James's army to form the celebrated Irish brigades of France and Austria.

From this time on the history of the Castle was that of successive Viceroys, few of whom were in any way notable, apart from giving their names to various Dublin streets and thoroughfares.

Dublin until the arrival of Ormonde had been largely contained within the limits of the old city walls. These walls were about 17 feet high, and between four and five feet thick, with towers at intervals from 16 to 40 feet high. Inside was a rampart, 15 feet thick, with buttresses at some points. The city gates were also strong and imposing. This was the city that was still besieged as late as 1649. But now though some citizens were unhappy about it, the city burst these bounds and began to spread out to the east and south.

The castle was visited in 1698 by John Dunton. 'The house was handsome but not magnificent. The rooms of state were on the first floor, approached by a noble staircase; below there was a large stone gallery. Behind the house a broad wall stretched the whole length of the building and from it a stone arch over a little river gave access to the garden by two spacious pairs of stairs.'

A vignette of the castle on Brooking's map of Dublin made in 1728 shows Robinson's range as it was rebuilt between 1710 and 1716 by Thomas Burgh, his successor as Surveyor General.

* * *

The British policy was once again aimed at the penalisation of Irish Catholics. But law was one thing, reality another. The long list of martyrs (aside from two murders) ended with the execution of St Oliver Plunkett, a victim of political intrigue by Titus Oates, in 1680. The active persecution of Catholics ended with

management prevented any rising in Ireland as a counterpart to the Scottish '45. When asked for reports of Catholic plots that had come to his attention, he

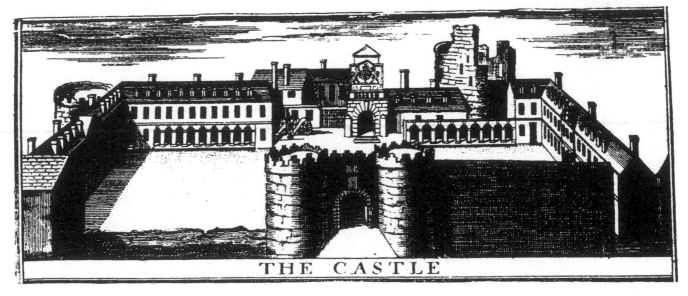

THE CASTLE

ABOVE: *Dublin Castle, as drawn by Charles Brooking in 1728, showing the almost ruinous state of parts of the fabric*

the death of Queen Anne in 1714. Dublin remained largely a Catholic city, though the Mass houses were down quiet back streets. Yet they did exist and as the Jacobite threat against the British state faded away, especially after the failed risings of 1715 and 1745, tolerance was more common, and the remaining legal and social disadvantages began to ameliorate. This was the end of the true penal era, though Catholic Emancipation did not come in full until 1829.

But in the eighteenth century the establishment in Dublin Castle was stoutly Protestant. The Viceroys were on the whole an undistinguished gallery, as their portraits that hang about the corners of the Castle today all too often suggest.

There were exceptions. One was the Earl of Pembroke, scion of a famous family, a member of the French Academy, to whom the philosopher John Locke dedicated his seminal *Essay on Human Understanding* (1690). Another was John, Lord Carteret (in Dublin in 1724 and 1727), who later became Prime Minister in England. And then there was Lord Chesterfield (1745), perhaps the most courtier-like figure of the day. He was idolised by the city and lived in great style. His political

reported to the Prime Minister that Miss Ambrose, a noted beauty of the day in Dublin, was the only 'dangerous papist' he had encountered.

It was Chesterfield, incidentally, who laid out the walks through the royal park outside Dublin, where Ormonde had begun the keeping of deer. Its Gaelic name, Fionn Uisce, did not appeal to a man of his classical temper, and he transformed it into the homonous Phoenix Park, symbolic – some thought – of a renewal of life in Ireland. Indeed, after the failure of that last Jacobite attempt to regain the throne, the harsher penal laws began to wither away and Catholics were able to practise their faith more openly. At Dublin Castle there were changes too. Chesterfield improved the place, building the present St Patrick's Hall. The modern Castle was beginning to emerge from its medieval chrysalis.

The Victorian novelist J.S. Le Fanu gives a vivid account of a reception at Dublin Castle which later brings on stage both Jonathan Swift and the essayist Joseph Addison, then secretary of the Lord Lieutenant. The year 1709 was the time of the vice-royalty of Thomas Wharton, Earl of Wharton.

AN EVENING AT THE CASTLE IN 1710

It was arranged, therefore, that the young lady, under the protection of Lady Stukely, and accompanied by Lord Aspenly and Henry Aswoode, should attend the first drawing-room at the castle, a ceremonial which had been fixed to take place a few days subsequently to the arrival of Lord Aspenly at Morley Court. Those who have seen the castle of Dublin only as it now stands, have beheld but the creation of the last sixty or seventy years, with the exception only of the wardrobe tower, an old gray cylindar of masonry, very dingy and dirty, which appears to have gone into half mourning for its departed companions, and presents something of the imposing character of an overgrown, mouldy band-box. At the beginning of the last century, however, matters were very different. The trim brick buildings with their spacious windows and symmetrical regularity of structure, which now complete the quadrangles of the castle, had not yet appeared; but in their stead masses of building, constructed with very little attention to architectural precision, either in their individual formation or in their relative position, stood ranged together, so as to form two irregular and gloomy squares. That portion of the building which was set apart for state occasions and the viceregal residence had undergone so many repairs and modifications, that very little if any of it could have been recognised by its original builder. Not so, however, with other portions of the pile: the ponderous old towers which have since disappeared, with their narrow loopholes and iron studded doors looming darkly over the less massive fabric of the place with stern and gloomy prospect, reminded the passer every moment, that the building, whose courts he trod, was not merely the theatre of stately ceremonies, but a fortress and a prison.

The vice-royalty of the Earl of Wharton was within a few weeks of its abrupt termination; the approaching discomfiture of the Whigs was not, however, sufficiently clearly revealed, in the levées and drawing-rooms of the Whig Lord Lieutenant The castle-yards, therefore, upon the occasion in question, crowded to excess with the

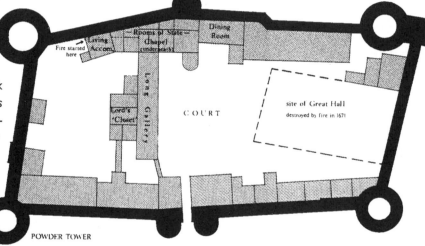

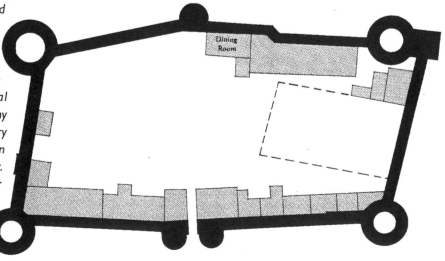

LEFT: *Plans of Dublin Castle, prepared by J.B. Maguire, of the Board of Works, who did much research into the history of 'Ireland's Bastille.'*

TOP: *based on a plan of 1673;*

BOTTOM: *after the fire in 1684*

gorgeous equipages in which the Irish aristocracy of the time delighted. The night had closed in unusual darkness, and the massive buildings, whose summits were buried in dense and black obscurity, were lighted only by the red reflected glow of crowded flambeaux and links – which, as the respective footmen who attended the crowding chairs and coaches, flourished them according to the approved fashion, scattered their wide showers of sparks into the eddying air, and illumined in a broad and ruddy glare, like that of a bonfire, the gorgeous equipages with which the square was now thronged, and the splendid figures which they successively discharged. There were coaches and four – out-riders – running footmen and hanging footmen – crushing and rushing – jostling and swearing – and burley coachmen with inflamed visages, lashing one another's horses and their own. Lackeys collaring and throttling one another, all 'for their master's honour', in the hot and disorderly dispute for precedence, and some even threatening an appeal to the swords – which, according to the barbarous fashion of the day, they carried, to the no small peril of the public and themselves. Others dragging the reins of strangers' horses, and backing them to make way for their own; – a proceeding which, of course, involved no small expenditure of blasphemy and vociferation. On the whole, it would not be easy to exaggerate the scene of riot and confusion which, under the very eye of the civil and military executive of the country was perpetually recurring, and that too ostensibly in honour of the supreme head of the Irish government.

RIGHT: *Schematic plan of Dublin Castle by Henry Pratt, 1708*

CHAPTER SEVEN

THE EIGHTEENTH CENTURY

There was much room for improvement at the Castle. With the settled times that existed for much of the eighteenth century, it took on the appearance which it largely retains to this day. It was in the Georgian era (1714–1829) that the Upper Yard was finished, together with the Bedford Tower and the State Apartments. A guidebook to Ireland published in 1779 reported that 'this castle is far superior to the palace of St. James's as well in the exterior, as the size and elegance of the apartments within'.

These improvements began when in 1710 the 2nd Duke of Ormonde (the grandson of the great Duke) obtained from the Treasury in London a grant of £3,000 to improve the approaches to the Castle. Two years later more money was granted for an arsenal, a Council Chamber and offices for the Receiver General. At this time the cross block was erected on the foundations of the thirteenth-century wall, between the Upper and Lower Yards, and it was here that the Council Chamber was placed, over the present archway (though the present block was reconstructed completely in 1961–4).

A court case some time later suggested that this scheme was halted in 1716, leaving unused stone that had been supplied. In Brooking's picture of 1728 some of this can be detected, for the castle there has the appearance of a medieval ruin with crumbling towers into which the modern block has been forced. On his plan the east range, where the Council Chamber was, is in deep shadow, but it must have matched the west range. The buildings were then two storeys high, with dormer windows. These were replaced by a full third storey in the nineteenth century. The west end of the

south range is incomplete: the unused stone must have been intended for this.

Dublin at this stage was a late medieval city of small size. It would enlarge greatly over the next century or so. Between the advent of William and Mary and George III there was little grand building in Dublin because of the political situation, although the city continued to expand. Dublin under the Georges, however, began to take on the appearance of the modern city, many of whose most distinguished buildings date from this era.

The next major figure associated with the Castle as Surveyor was Pearce. He was followed by Arthur Dobbs, who prepared estimates for building a new entrance on the site of the medieval gatehouse which can be seen in Brooking's drawing. In 1742 Dobbs was given permission to use £2,800 'for the charge of pulling down that part of the building in Dublin Castle which is propped with timber, where the Inner Office, Council Office, and the Chief Secretary's apartment and offices are kept and for rebuilding the same'. This, it seems, was the block on the north-east corner of the yard where the Powder Tower stood.

In 1746 Lord Chesterfield wrote that 'the Great Staircase, Battle Axe Hall (in the south range), Chaplain's Apartments and other necessary rooms comprising the Principal entrance into the castle are not only in a most ruinous condition but in immediate danger of falling to the ground although continually propped ... and all that space of ground between the said principal entrance and Bermingham's Tower containing one hundred and fifty four feet in depth, forming more than one half of the chief side

of the court of the said castle, nowe lieth as in one great ruin although necessary to be employed as well as for the Dignity as for the Convenience of His Majesty's Governors'.

He thought that the total cost of rebuilding might amount to £5,205. The money must have been forthcoming, for the work had been completed by 1753. In 1752 the handsome Bedford Tower in the Upper Yard, with the great gates on either side was erected. It was named after John Russell, the Duke of Bedford. Van Nost, the leading sculptor of the day in Ireland, was responsible for the huge leaden statues over them of Fortitude and Justice. This last was the subject of much political mockery then and later.

Statue of Justice, mark well her station,
Her face to the Castle, her back to the nation.

And unlike other statues of its type, her eyes were unveiled, too! The scales which she carried also used to fill with water, and become unbalanced. The authorities solved this little problem by having holes drilled in the pans.

The Castle's appearance then can be judged from a view by Tudor, in which can be seen the new Bedford Tower, erected over the old gate house, and the grand Entrance leading out into Dame Street.

The State Apartments at the Castle were renovated in 1746. The architect, Joseph Jarratt, claimed to have designed the new buildings, but it is thought more likely that his plans were based on designs by Pearce done in about 1730, soon after he had worked on the Houses of Parliament in College Green (now the Bank of Ireland) and Castletown House.

The Hall of the Castle was used as a ballroom. It appears in a picture of the period attributed to William van der Hagen, which shows a fashionable event of 4 November 1731. The New Hall (later St Patrick's Hall) was built some time after 1746.

In 1775 the fourteenth-century Bermingham Tower was demolished and re-erected in its present form. Its ancient base is, however, still retained within the modern fabric.

Running east from this on the foundations of the old Castle wall was the outer wall of St Patrick's Hall. In the 1790s Valdre rebuilt the north-east corner; and during the years between 1817 and 1828 further work was carried out by Francis Johnston.

The Wardrobe Tower (so called because it was here that the royal robe, the Cap of Maintenance and other 'furniture of state' had been preserved), now renamed the Record Tower, was renovated and the machiolated parapets, which are such a distinctive feature of it today, were added in 1819. The tower was

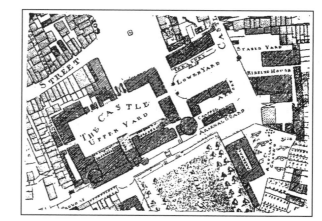

56 feet across with immensely thick walls. The registers were stored around the circular walls, while the reading room so long used by those researching the state papers was very small. But, of course, it was originally intended only for the use of the Chief Secretary's own small staff of clerks, and not for the general public of Ireland.

None of this work was particularly distinguished, and does not compare with the domestic works to be found elsewhere in the city and the country. The Lords Lieutenant were concerned to save money for the Treasury, and with good reason, for the Castle was used only for bi-annual meetings of the Irish Parliament which lasted about a week. No MPs lasted very long, and some never came to Ireland at all.

As John Cornforth observed: *'No one was under any illusion about the castle and what it stood for, but all the same it was the seat of the executive and the focus of social life in Ireland throughout the eighteenth century. Consequently, when one visits it today it is important to visualise it crowded with people who the Lord Lieutenant*

OPPOSITE: *Rocque's map of the ever-expanding Dublin, broken free of the old city bounds in the eighteenth century*

LEFT: *Detail of Dublin from Rocque's survey, 1756*

was trying to impress and appease, and who equally were trying to impress the Lord Lieutenant and get their petitions granted.'

The life at the viceregal court in the eighteenth century echoed the general life of Georgian Ireland. The model was, of course, the Court of St James, which by European standards was considered very formal. But to this state formality the little court in Dublin added touches of extravagance which are thought of as particularly Irish. Between 1758 and 1781 the Viceroys returned again to live in the Castle, leaving the King's House in Chapelizod to the military. It was not until 1781 that a new viceregal house was bought, the present lodge in Phoenix Park where the President of Ireland now lives.

Viscount Townshend (1767) made a new departure in the life of the court by gathering Irishmen around him. At first he had a Scottish secretary, but in 1769 he changed him for Sir George Macartney, a brilliant man who had been envoy to the court of Catherine the Great in Russia, and would later travel into China to face the Chinese Emperor. But Macartney, like Jephson the master of horse, and Dennis the chaplain (a college friend of Burke), were Anglo-Irishmen to a later generation (though this distinction did not then exist), Irish meaning for Londoners a Protestant native of Ireland. The other kind of Irish were not quite so acceptable, pace Miss Ambrose.

Townshend made a tour of southern Ireland, visiting in turn Limerick, Killarney and Cork, and taking with him the antiquarian General Vallency, whose ideas about Irish antiquity were once so fruitful and are now so mocked. He passed his summers at Leixlip castle.

There and at Dublin social life reached new heights. The social season in the early part of the year was inaugurated and with it the St Patrick's Ball.

It was an era of fancy dress balls and amateur theatricals in Dublin and the provinces. During the tenure of Lord Carlisle, Miss Herbert wrote to a friend in London in April 1782: *'We outdo you in dissipation ... Nothing can be so gay as Dublin is – the Castle twice a week, the opera twice a week, with plays, assemblies and suppers to fill up the time.'*

Even greater festivities marked the inauguration of the Order of St Patrick by George III in 1783. The first investiture of Knights was held in St Patrick's Cathedral (where some of the Knights' banners are still hung), and was followed by a great banquet in St Patrick's Hall.

As the National Order for Ireland, the Order of St Patrick consisted of the King and twenty-two Knights Companion. It was modelled on the Order of the Garter and, like that earlier order, the insignia consisted of a Collar, Star and Badge. The motto of the Order was *Quis separabit* ('Who shall separate [us]?') It was seen as a way of securing loyalty to the crown in a country where patriotism, albeit Protestant patriotism, was on the rise. (It was the Order that established the Cross of St Patrick – perhaps derived from the banner of the Geraldines – as the national emblem of Ireland which was later incorporated into the Union flag.)

The next year saw the arrival of the Duke of Rutland, who opposed the taxation of the American colonies, that unfortunate piece of legislation that precipitated the great Age of Revolution. He did little in the way of introducing new government measures, but he entertained lavishly, and was the first of the Viceroys to live in the Viceregal Lodge in Phoenix Park.

Rutland was an inebriate of a jolly kind. He breakfasted on six turkey eggs and ended each day with a drinking party. During a tour of Westmeath in 1787 he was forced to put up for the night in Thomas Cuffe's inn in Kilbeggan. The Viceroy was taken with his host's fund of funny Irish stories and, to show his appreciation at the end of a long night's drinking, insisted on knighting him. Alas, dawn brought sobriety. Cuffe was called in, and offered any amount of money to give up his title. He was willing enough to please his Lordship, but 'Her Ladyship says I mustn't'. The poor dissipated Duke died in 1787, and was waked for several days and nights in the old Irish House of Lords. He gave his name to a memorial in Merrion Square, the Rutland Fountain, from which the poor of Dublin might drink – water!

The American Revolution brought about a change in Irish life with the establishment of the National Volunteers, and the wresting away from London of the legislative independence of Ireland in 1782. The

Castleknock Light Dragoons, part of that movement under the command of their colonel, Luke Gardiner, were reported by the *Dublin Evening Post* on 26 October 1779 to be drilling in the Lower Castle Yard, beneath the very windows of the government's officials. This was a week before the historic parade of the Irish Volunteers on College Green, which was the subject of a famous painting by Francis Wheatley which shows Gardiner among the officers, on a mettlesome mount, with his sabre drawn in salute.

With the independence of the Irish Parliament under Grattan and the appointment as Viceroy of Lord Fitzwilliam, conciliation made a move forward in Ireland. But his recall to London in 1795 was (as Lecky pointed out) a serious error. Catholic Emancipation was delayed for another thirty years. Worse followed in 1798. It was at this time, towards the last years of the eighteenth century, that the odious reputation of Dublin Castle in the minds of the 'mere Irish' can be remarked.

The Rising of 1798 (much influenced by the hopes and fears of the French, rather than the American, Revolution) saw appalling things done. The excesses of the Yeomanry – the Ancient Briton regiment from Wales, and the Hessian mercenaries hired from a minor German kingdom, recruited to fill out the army, were particularly bad.

Sir Jonah Barrington in his highly personal history of the events of the day, *The Rise and Fall of the Irish Nation*, gives a vivid impression of the scene at the Castle itself:

'Some dead bodies of insurgents, sabred the night before by Lord Roden's dragoons, were brought in a cart to Dublin, with some prisoners tied together: the carcasses were stretched out in the Castle-yard, where the Viceroy then resided, and in full view of the Secretary's windows: they lay on the pavement as trophies of the first skirmish, during a hot day, cut and gashed in every part, covered with clotted blood and dust, the most frightful spectacle which ever disgraced a royal residence save the seraglio.

'After several hours' exposure, some appearance of life was perceived in one of the mutilated carcasses. The man had been stabbed and gashed in various parts; his body was removed into the guard-room and means were taken to restore animation; efforts succeeded, he entirely recovered and was pardoned by Lord Camden; he was an extraordinarily fine young man, above six feet high, the son of a Mr. Keough, an opulent landholder of Rathfarnham; he did not, however, change his principles and was, ultimately, sent out of the country.'

LEFT: *Henry Grattan speaking before the Irish Parliament during its brief years of legislative independence*

Lord Cornwallis, who had carried the day in India, but been defeated in the American colonies, was the general who had the task firstly of suppressing the Rebellion and then of carrying through the Act of Union. This was done by wholesale bribery and corruption – many now-respected Irish titles date from this shameful episode. In 1801 George III (the supposedly 'mad King George' who had already lost the American colonies) signed the Act of Union, but he stoutly refused to agree to the emancipation of his Catholic subjects in the three realms, which was to have come with the Act.

With the Union, a new era and a new century began. But the struggle for the national destiny of Ireland entered a new phase.

AN IMPRESSION OF THE CASTLE IN 1798

Friday the 18th day of May, 1798. The City of Dublin was proclaimed to be in a state of disturbance according to the provisions of that ever to be remembered act called 'The Insurrection Act.' This appeared to every man acquainted with party secrets a most unnecessary exertion of that extraordinary power with which the Government was invested, in confidence that it would be resorted to only when it was manifestly certain that the regular laws were inadequate to the preservation of

long disgraced the city, was rarely met with — in the interval of business an almost universal silence seemed to pervade the streets. However, it was a dread calm such as often precedes a storm — those at the helm saw this and adopted the above measure as one precaution — the sequel of events, contrary to the representations of the interested and expectations of many sensible men, Government are found fully justified.

Saturday the 19th — I did not go out into the streets until evening. When I approached the Castle I

RIGHT: *The arrest of Lord Edward Fitzgerald, as imagined by the artist George Cruikshank*

order, and the protection of the lives and properties of his Majesty's loyal subjects. Now it is remarkable that the city of Dublin never presented such a face of tranquillity in the ordinary times of peace — not a house or a street robbery to be heard of — an instance of drunkenness, that once almost inveterate cause of riot and disorder which

found its avenues guarded and nobody permitted to pass: the guards told me there was a prisoner there under examination. I passed on without much anxiety, and in the course of the evening I heard a report of the capture of Lord Edward Fitzgerald, to which I gave little credit or attention. Sunday morning I soon learned the fate of Lord

Edward and that he was at the Castle the evening before when I passed it. The public mind seemed much agitated – the countenances of some expressed great grief, a few open joy, but most were serious. The yeomanry were reviewed in different quarters of the town, and paraded the streets in great numbers. There was but one subject of conversation and that was the unfortunate Lord Edward. From the commencement of the war he appeared the declared opponent of Government, and the champion of the independence of this country – some say he took a lesson in politics from his lady Pamela, said to be a daughter of that unnatural and detested monster Egalité [Philippe Egalité, Duke of Orleans] – Lord Edward, whom I have often seen, was in the middle size and of hardy make, like Flint – his engaging countenance was good natured as well as enterprising – he was remarkable for dressing like an English groom or, as we are told, like a French Jacobin – a member of a beloved and illustrious family. He was well fitted for a leader of the people in the approaching struggle and now from his general conduct in life and his heroic conduct when taken he was loved and revered by his friends and respected and pitied by his enemies – the capture of Lord Edward was justly esteemed as fortunate by the Loyalists and it seemed to cast an universal gloom over the United Men this evening. I supped in Murray's in Great George's Street where, as I was accustomed, I expected to meet a pleasant party – but nothing could raise the dejected spirits of this party – the females were in tears all day – and in entertainment it is not the province of men to take the lead.

from The Diary of Richard Farrell Barrister-at-Law (1798), *ed. Dr George A. Little*

RIGHT: *Dublin
Castle with some of
the garrison, about
1843, by the Rev.
Calvert Jones —
one of the very first
photographs ever
taken in Dublin
(see page 70)*

CHAPTER EIGHT

THE EARLY NINETEENTH CENTURY

The Act of Union, passed by the use of almost whole-sale bribery, came into force in 1801. And it was to break this union, either by constitutional means or by physical force, that the following generations of Irish nationalists dedicated themselves.

The first attempt was made after only two years by Robert Emmet – 'Bold Robert Emmet, the darlin' of Ireland' – in 1803. In that year the Yeomanry, who were used to patrol and police the Irish countryside, cost £100,000 a month. Emmet intended to seize the Castle, but his plans mis-carried and only a handful of insurgents turned out. In the Rising, little more than a street fracas, Lord Kilwarden, the Irish Lord Chief Justice, was dragged from his carriage and mur-dered. The public execu-tion of Robert Emmet, who had been incarcerated in the Record Tower in Dublin Castle, took place outside St Catherine's church, where he was hanged and beheaded. Where he was buried is now unknown, as his body was removed from Bully's Acre, behind Kilmainham, where it was first laid.

Ironically, the records of his rebellion – as well as that of Lord Edward Fitzgerald – were later stored in the room he had been kept in. The romantic outpourings of these young men were bundled up with the reports of the informers who had betrayed them.

BELOW: *The murder of Lord Kilwarden during the Rising of 1803, engraving by George Cruikshank*

It was in the same tower that his unfortunate ser-vant, Anne Devlin, was detained and tortured, though she staunchly never revealed the secrets of the rebellion.

An Encounter with Town Major Sirr in 1837

The poet and novelist Katharine Tynan recalls in her memoirs an incident from the childhood of her father, later a farmer in County Dublin, who was born in Dublin in 1829.

Although the actual place of his birth was an old Dublin street under the shadow of Dublin Castle walls ... he said he went to school in Hoey's Court, off Werburgh Street, the very school which boasted Dean Swift as a scholar. Round about the spot where he was born the streets are storied: the very stones cry the names and fates of Irish patriots. In St Werburgh's Church, close to where he was born, the brothers Sheares were buried. Practically the whole bloody history of Ireland under English occupation has Dublin Castle as its centre. As one goes up and down those dark streets — they are lighter now than they were in my girlhood or his boyhood — what shades elbow each other! Tragical shades! If you are interested in the social side of Dublin life, you look for your ghosts about the old Parliament Houses and Trinity College. In College Green was Daly's Club-House, where all the wits and beaux and swashbucklers and fine gentlemen of every sort congregated in the brilliant years of the eighteenth century that led up to the débâcle of the Rebellion. About Dublin Castle the memories are mostly sombre.

There is an aura, the environing light of patriots and martyrs, in those streets. Impossible, one would say, for a child of imagination to grow up there anything but a patriot.

His mind in later years was an epitome of old Dublin. You could scarcely talk of any famous person or happening that it would not set him off on a reminiscence ... He had all sorts of memories of the Dublin of his youth. One curious link with the past was that he remembered how Major Sirr — hated in Ireland as the man who captured and mortally wounded Lord Edward Fitzgerald, the bright, the beautiful, the immortally young — had patted his curly locks as a child. His evidence about Major Sirr was rather in the direction of rehabilitating him. He was never one for conventional beliefs; and while he yielded to none in his love for Lord Edward, he was not the less impartial as regards him whom many people would have called Lord Edward's murderer.

'When I was a flaxen-haired child,' he said, 'I used to play about the Castle Yard. One day we had been playing marbles on the steps of a house, when the door opened, and a man whom I took to be a tall man hurriedly came out. My companions scattered, but I remained. He took me by the chin, and lifting it up looked down into my eyes. "Well, little boy, do you often play marbles on my steps?" he asked. "Very often," I said fearlessly. "And hop-scotch, and spinning tops, and all your other games?" "Yes, sir." "Well, you can go on playing them then, and don't be afraid." After he was gone, the others, running back cried out: "Did you know it was Major Sirr?" I had no idea indeed that it was he whose name was something of a bugaboo to frighten children in the dark.'

Hated as he was, however, he had the reputation, as a magistrate, of being fair and impartial.

Katharine Tynan,
Twenty-five Years (1913)

BELOW: *Making pikes in a secret workshop in preparation for Emmet's rising in 1803, as imagined by the artist George Cruikshank*

Dublin in 1806) give some idea of the high revelry of late Georgian Ireland. Lady Morgan, author of The Wild Irish Girl (1806), told how the ladies of the Court would race around the halls of the Castle playing 'Catch-as-Catch-Who'; though later Lord William Lennox denied the truth of this charming picture.

LEFT: Woodcut of the Upper Castle Yard in 1830s

Sir Arthur Wellesley, later the Duke of Wellington, was Chief Secretary in Richmond's time. His elder brother, Marquess Wellesley, was twice Lord Lieutenant. Having lived and ruled in India, Lord

BELOW LEFT: Plan of the Castle area prepared by the Wide Streets Commissioners

Henry Charles Sirr had actually been born in Dublin Castle, where his father was town-major, or chief of the city police, on 25 November 1764. Having been both a soldier and a wine merchant, he was appointed acting town-major in 1798, after acting the post for two years. He was given an official residence inside Dublin Castle. On 19 May 1798 he was one of those who captured Lord Edward Fitzgerald in the house in Thomas Street where he had been hiding since March, and in 1803 he also organised the arrest of Robert Emmet at Harold's Cross. Sirr retired (on full pay) in 1826, but was allowed to go on living in his home in Dublin Castle, where he died on 7 January 1841.

It is an odd scene, though, these Dublin urchins playing about in the Upper Castle Yard, unfazed by the dignitaries passing to and fro.

* * *

The representatives of the king were now strictly Lords Lieutenant, but were still called Viceroys. The Duke of Richmond (1807–13) not only entertained in season with great lavishness, but also lived constantly in Ireland, providing some sort of counter-pull to those who had flocked away to London now that the Lords and Commons of Ireland sat there.

The hectic novels of Charles Lever (born in

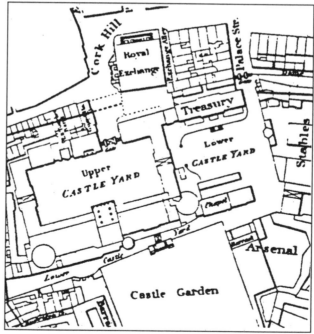

Wellesley lived in great state far beyond his means. He was married twice. His second wife, in 1826, was a beautiful American widow, Mrs Mary Patterson, a Catholic, who by one of those odd chances of history,

was connected by marriage with the Bonaparte family. Madame Bonaparte wrote to a friend about Mary's good fortune.

He is 66 years old; so much in debt that the plate on his table is hired; had his carriages once seized in the streets of Dublin; and has a great part of his salary mortgaged. But with all these drawbacks he is considered a very great match, owing to his rank.

Every Sunday the marchioness would drive out of the Viceregal Lodge with an escort of cavalry to attend Mass in the Pro-cathedral in Marlborough Street.

* * *

In the ordinary way the Viceroys attended religious services in the Castle chapel. At this time, however, they went to St Werburgh's, the Church of Ireland parish church at the rear of the Castle. The old Castle chapel had been demolished, and on 15 February 1807, the foundation stone of a new one was laid. Eventually costing some £42,000, it was designed by Francis Johnston and was eventually dedicated in 1814, being first used for services on Christmas Day. Though the interior had the appearance of being plain Portland stone, it was actually made of painted plaster and wood. The chapel was dominated by a an enormous pulpit, now removed to St Werburgh's. The exterior is decorated with a curious range of carved heads by Edward Smythe (famous for the riverine heads on the Custom House) and his son. An engraving of 1816, by James del Veccio, shows the new chapel, facing the Treasury building across the Lower Yard, and behind it the Ordnance Office, with the avenue leading away to the gate at Great Ship Street.

George IV kept Court at Dublin Castle when he visited Ireland during the term of Earl Talbot as Viceroy in 1821. The King is said to have been hardly sober during the entire visit, which was, nevertheless, of some significance, as there had been no royal visit to Ireland since the time of William and Mary. It was then that he began the custom, kept up by Lords Lieutenant until towards the end of British rule in Ireland, of kissing the young ladies on their first presentation at court.

The salary of the Viceroy had risen from a mere

£100 in the days of Sidney to £30,000 at the time of the Marquess of Anglesey. Anglesey, a wealthy man, gave back £10,000, after which the Treasury (ever careful with the public purse) reduced all later salaries by that amount. When he left Ireland the Marquess invited all his Dublin tradesmen to come to London as his guests, to stay in Northumberland House and see the sights. The good men enjoyed their stay, but were nearly ruined by the cost of tipping.

* * *

With the Act of Union, which made Ireland part of the United Kingdom, Dublin Castle was elevated into the main centre of the government administration. In those days this was no very grand matter, but as the century progressed the civil service grew and the operations of government in all areas became more complex. This was especially so after Catholic Emancipation in 1829, and the Reform Act of 1837.

In 1836 the Irish Constabulary (later, after 1867, the Royal Irish Constabulary) was organised as a gendarmerie or carabinieri to police the rural districts. Armed rural police had been commonplace in Europe since the end of the eighteenth century, but they were not the norm in Britain. In this, as in so many other things, Ireland was different. Their headquarters was in Dublin Castle, with the older Dublin Metropolitan Police. From barracks manned by a sergeant and a handful of constables, the whole island was patrolled. The recruits were, of course, drawn from the general population, and at most times the majority of the population were glad of them. Ireland, apart from agrarian 'outrages', was a country remarkably free of true crime, hence much of the work of the RIC was political in nature. Though they had little trouble in dealing with the Fenians in 1867, the RIC were not truly a fighting force. Though, as one Chief Secretary remarked, they had Ireland under the microscope, they were to prove no match for the IRA of a later generation. But for most of the nineteenth century they were an essential element in the Castle rule of Ireland.

Since 1802 the maintenance of all the government buildings around the Castle and the city had been in the hands of the original Board of Works. This included not

OPPOSITE: *Interior of Francis Johnston's third Chapel Royal in the 1960s – the flags are those of Irish regiments in the French service*

only Kilmainham and Phoenix Park, for instance, but also the erection of the Chapel Royal, and in 1836 the adaptation of the Treasury Buildings in the Lower Yard for use by the Irish Constabulary. All the later work to this day was done by the Board or its successor, the Office of Public Works. It was their skill that created and preserved what we can see today – when they could get the money out of the government of the day!

* * *

Only a few years after the invention of photography, the very first photographs made in Ireland featured Dublin Castle. They were the work of the Rev. Calvert Jones, a friend of Fox Talbot, the inventor of the photographic negative, who visited the city in about 1846 and made a series of now much-admired pictures (though for a long time they were thought to have been Fox Talbot's own work).

Here are the streets and scenes of early Victorian Dublin, with its handsome buildings, well-dressed folk, and streets sullied by dung. Along with the Bank of Ireland, St George's Church, the Wellington Monument and Trinity College, he also photographed the Upper Yard at the Castle, recording a group of soldiers and perhaps a senior civil servant in an elegant set-piece before the backdrop of the Bedford Tower. With their redcoats and stovepipe hats, these people represent the rulers of Ireland on the eve of the Famine.

CHAPTER NINE

THE CASTLE, THE FAMINE AND NEW IRELAND

In Dublin Castle the administration of Ireland was all too often in the hands of Englishmen. It was shown at its most ineffective during the dark days of the Famine, especially in 1847 and after. With millions starving, dying and fleeing the country, the government's response was seen to be quite inadequate, even for those days of non-intervention. The administration suffered a species of breakdown or stroke, in which the accumulation of events caused a brain clot at Dublin Castle.

Indeed, many of those at the Castle Court were more concerned with the long illness of the Lord Lieutenant, Lord Bessborough, who died of 'dropsy of the chest' on 16 May 1847. Though he had been widely admired in official circles 'it was sad to hear the ladies wishing him dead that the gaieties might recommence, and the young A.D.C.s fearing not to be 'clear' in time for the Derby'.

Though the Viceroy and the Chief Secretary were well aware of the situation, it was impossible to move either Lord John Russell, the Prime Minister, or Charles Trevelyan, the permanent head of the Treasury in London. Their belief that 'private enterprise' must be the key to any relief effort allowed millions to die of starvation and disease, or to emigrate with hearts filled with hatred.

For the next seventy-five years it would be a prolonged struggle to cast off the dead hand of Dublin Castle on Irish affairs. What many English people, dedicated to their own sense of liberty, seem not to have

LEFT: *A scene of death and lamentation during the famine*
ILLUSTRATED LONDON NEWS

realised was just how centralised the government of Ireland was by comparison with the rest of the United Kingdom. Scotland had its own special legal and educational system, while the counties and cities of England and Wales enjoyed a great deal of local government. But in Ireland everything was run from the departments of the Castle. In England, the Home Secretary had control only over the Metropolitan police in London; the local constabularies were all separate and independent. But in Ireland the Chief Secretary ran the Dublin police, the RIC and the secret services, as well as all the other affairs of public life.

For Irish Nationalists, Dublin Castle was shorthand for all that they found wrong with Ireland, resentments that from time to time broke out into actual rebellion, as in 1848 when the leaders of Young Ireland attempted a failed coup. The police spies who had been active in earlier times became even more important, especially after 1859 with the rise of the Fenians. The Rising of 1867 seemed to be the end of that menace. After the miscarried rising which ended in the rout after the Battle of Tallaght in the snow of March 1867, hundreds of Fenians were arrested all over the city, and herded into the Upper Castle Yard, where they were penned while being processed by the police. It was one of the most extraordinary sights that the Castle had ever seen.

But just as the Young Ireland and 1798 had been an inspiration for the Fenians, so the Fenians became an inspiration to following generations. The Castle was an anachronism.

* * *

QUEEN VICTORIA WRITES HOME

Lodge, Phoenix Park, 6th August 1849

Though this letter will only go to-morrow I will begin it to-day and tell you that everything has gone off beautifully since we arrived in Ireland, and that our entrance into Dublin was really a magnificent thing. By my letter to Louise you will have heard of our arrival in the Cove of Cork. Our visit to Cork was very successful; the Mayor was knighted on deck (on board the Fairy), like in times of old. Cork is about seventeen miles up the River Lee, which is beautifully wooded and reminds us of Devonshire scenery. We had previously stepped on shore at Cove, a small place, to enable them to call it Queen's Town; the enthusiasm is immense, and at Cork there was more firing than I remember since the Rhine.

We left Cork with fair weather, but a head sea and contrary wind which made it rough and me very sick.

7th. – I was unable to continue till now, and have since received your kind letter, for which I return my warmest thanks. We went into Waterford Harbour on Saturday afternoon, which is likewise a fine, large, safe harbour. Albert went up to Waterford in the Fairy, but I did not. The next morning we received much the same report of the weather which we had done at Cork, viz. that the weather was fair but the wind contrary. However we went out, as it could not be helped, and we might have remained there some days for no use. The first three hours were very nasty, but afterwards it cleared and the evening was beautiful. The entrance at seven o'clock into Kingston Harbour was splendid; we came in with ten steamers, and the whole harbour, wharf, and every surrounding place was covered with thousands and thousands of people, who received us with the greatest enthusiasm. We disembarked yesterday morning at ten o'clock, and took two hours to come here. The most perfect order was maintained in spite of the immense mass of people assembled, and a more good-humoured crowd I never saw, but noisy and excitable beyond belief, talking, jumping, and shrieking instead of cheering. There were numbers of troops out, and it really was a wonderful scene. This is a very pretty place, and the house reminds me of dear Claremont. The view of the Wicklow Mountains from the windows is very beautiful, and the whole park is very extensive and full of very fine trees.

We drove out yesterday afternoon and were followed by jaunting-cars and riders and people running and screaming, which would have amused you. In the evening we had a dinner party, and so we have to-night. This morning we visited the Bank, the Model School (where the Protestant and Catholic Archbishops received us), and the College, and this afternoon we went to the Military Hospital. To-morrow we have a Levée, where 1,700 are to be presented, and the next day a Review, and in the evening the Drawing-Room, when 300 ladies are to be presented.

George is here, and has a command here. He rode on one side of our carriage yesterday. You see more ragged a wretched people here than I ever saw anywhere else. En revanche, the women are really very handsome – quite in the lowest class – as well at Cork as here; such beautiful black eyes and hair and such fine colours and teeth.

I must now take my leave. Ever your most affectionate Niece,

Victoria R.

But some found the anachronism delightful. On 28 May 1852, Archibald William, Earl of Eglinton and Winton, was appointed Viceroy. A liberal patron of all kinds of manly sports, from horse racing to quoits, he was famous (or perhaps notorious) as the organiser of the Eglinton Tournament in 1839. This was to have been a revival of medieval jousting, a romantic throwback to the great age of chivalry, and though guests came from all over to his Scottish estate, the event was rained off. His appointment in February 1852 was made the butt of jokes in *Punch*; but, his biographer observes, '*Everyone lived to eat their words for he proved to be the best Viceroy there had been in a generation*'.

His wife was a shrew with whom he did not get on. During one official Drawing Room his diary records that he embraced 930 ladies in an evening. This was more than his wife could bear, and she was once heard to mutter 'It is too much'. She died soon after, and during his second term in 1858 he fell in love with the eldest daughter of Lord Essex, Adela Capel, with whom

RIGHT: *Eviction
scene during the
Land War of 1880*

he had two happy years before her death in child-birth. Great extravagance marked his two terms of office. Special care was given to having magnificent carriages and splendid horses. Whether this was fully appreciated by everyone in impoverished Ireland is doubtful. Certainly he left to his heirs enormous debts from his terms as Viceroy of Ireland when he died in 1861.

The two terms of office of the 'popular but eccentric' Lord Carlisle (in 1855–8 and 1859–64) found Dublin Castle the scene of endless theatricals. He had been a supporter of the Reform Act, and as Chief Secretary for Ireland (1835–41) had introduced the Irish Tithe, Irish Municipal Reform and Poor Law Bills. During his time as Viceroy he devoted himself to the improvement of Irish agriculture and manufacturing.

It was at this time that Donnybrook Fair, established by a Royal Patent in early Norman days, was bought out and abolished. The city of Dublin had grown too respectable, or at least Donnybrook had, in true Victorian style, and the scenes of drunken debauchery were not welcome to the refined tastes of the day.

The Duke of Abercorn (1866 and 1874) lived in an almost regal style. His daughters – one of whom was the Corsande of Benjamin Disraeli's contemporary novel of society manners, Lothair (1870) – had been beauties of London society. It was during his time that the splendid ceremonial of the Investiture of a Knight of St Patrick, which had been held from time to time in St Patrick's Cathedral, was transferred to St Patrick's Hall in the Castle itself.

Abercorn was followed by John Churchill, Duke of Marlborough (in 1876), and by Francis de Grey, Earl Cowper (1880–82) – both now recalled by most people only from the suburban roads to which they gave their names. Whatever the Viceroys attempted to do, they came and went so rapidly that they had little real impact on the country. The governance of Ireland lay in the hands of the permanent Under Secretary for Ireland. For much of this period, this was Thomas Henry Burke.

In 1879 the crops failed and Ireland was threatened with a famine. Land agitation spread across the country with the rise of the Land League. The administrative reaction to this was in the hands of Burke. Born in 1829, he was a Catholic, the son of an impoverished Galway landlord. Through his mother he was a great-nephew of Cardinal Wiseman. He entered government service in 1849, at the end of the Famine, and became successively private secretary to Sir Thomas Reddington, Edward Cardwell, Sir Robert Peel and Lord Carlingford. He was appointed Under Secretary for Ireland in 1869. He was in effect the permanent Irish Civil Service, the man who remained en place while English politicians came and went on the mail boat. In the eyes of advanced Republicans, Burke was the evil genius of British rule in Ireland. Worse, his being a well-connected Catholic made him a double traitor. As Chief Secretary for Ireland, Forster attempted to coerce the nation, eventually detaining Parnell and many other leaders in Kilmainham. Eventually a settlement was reached with the government ('The Kilmainham Treaty') in April 1882. Cowper and Forster resigned; and Earl Spencer and Lord Frederick Cavendish were appointed by the Gladstone government as the new Viceroy and Chief Secretary. On 2 May Parnell and others were released.

On 6 May, Earl Spencer and Lord Frederick Cavendish arrived in Dublin, and the Viceroy was installed in Dublin Castle. After the ceremony Cavendish and Burke, while walking back to their official residences in Phoenix Park, were assassinated by a group of men armed with surgical knives.

Such were the high expectations of the day that the shock of this crime rocked Europe. Its repercussions on Irish politics persisted until the 1930s. The culprits were eventually arrested through the services of an informer. They were exposed as a radical Fenian splinter group called the Invincibles, one of whose main leaders was a Dublin town councillor named Carey.

The police officer in charge of the investigation was Inspector Mallon, who was based in Dublin Castle, and it was also in a small room in Dublin Castle (actually in a house in Exchange Court) that the magistrate John Adye Curran conducted the hearings of the Commission that delved into the dark depths of this crime. On 13 January 1883, the first of some twenty-seven were arrested. The trials produced extraordinary revelations, the least of which came from Carey, the leader of the group, who turned Queen's evidence. He escaped with his life, but five men were hanged. While travelling to a new life in South Africa, Carey was assassinated at sea.

The good reputation of Dublin Castle was reinforced by this episode. In the aftermath a failed attempt was made in April 1884 to bomb Ship Street barracks at the rear of the castle – the device exploded harmlessly. The administration might be open to attack, but through both the police and the courts they would bring the culprits to justice – even though, as in the case of the equally notorious Maamtrasna murders, they would sometimes hang the wrong man. The Phoenix Park murders were not the only matter that drew the eyes of the world to Dublin Castle, for nationalists seized every opportunity to show the Castle in a different light.

On 25 August 1883 the Nationalist newspaper

ABOVE RIGHT:

Thomas Henry Burke, Permanent Under Secretary for Ireland, murdered in the Phoenix Park, May 1882, by the Invincibles
WINDSOR MAGAZINE

RIGHT: *The room in the Detective Office in which Judge John Adye Curran conducted his inquisition of the Invincibles*
WINDSOR MAGAZINE

BY THE LORD LIEUTENANT OF IRELAND.

A PROCLAMATION.

COWPER.

WHEREAS an Association styling itself " THE IRISH NATIONAL LAND LEAGUE" has existed for some time past, assuming to interfere with the Queen's subjects in the free exercise of their lawful rights, and especially to control the relations of Landlords and Tenants in Ireland :

AND WHEREAS the designs of the said Association have been sought to be effected by an organized system of intimidation ; attempting to obstruct the service of Process and execution of the Queen's Writs, and seeking to deter the Queen's subjects from fulfilling their contracts and following their lawful callings and occupations :

AND WHEREAS the said Association has now avowed its purpose to be to prevent the payment of all Rent, and to effect the subversion of the Law as administered in the Queen's name in Ireland :

NOW WE hereby warn all persons that the said Association styling itself "The Irish National Land League," or by whatsoever other name it may be called or known, is an unlawful and criminal Association ; and that all Meetings and Assemblies to carry out or promote its designs or purposes are alike unlawful and criminal, and will be prevented and, if necessary, dispersed by force.

AND WE, do hereby warn all subjects of Her Majesty the Queen, who may have become connected with the said Association, to disconnect themselves therefrom, and abstain from giving further countenance thereto.

AND WE do hereby make known that all the powers and resources at Our command will be employed to protect the Queen's subjects in Ireland, in the free exercise of their lawful rights, and the peaceful pursuit of their lawful callings and occupations ; to enforce the fulfilment of all lawful obligations, and to save the process of the Law and the execution of the Queen's Writs from hindrance or obstruction.

AND WE do hereby call on all loyal and well-affected subjects of the Crown to aid Us in upholding and maintaining the authority of the Law, and the Supremacy of the Queen in this Her Realm of Ireland.

Dated at Dublin Castle, this Twentieth day of October, 1881.

By His Excellency's Command,

W. E. FORSTER.

GOD SAVE THE QUEEN.

DUBLIN: PRINTED BY FREDERICK PILKINGTON, 87, 88, and 89, ABBEY STREET, PRINTER TO THE QUEEN'S MOST EXCELLENT MAJESTY.

RIGHT: *Official government proclamation issued from Dublin Castle during the Land War, over the signature of W.E. ('Buckshot') Forster*

United Ireland published for the first time allegations against County Inspector James Ellis French, who was the director of the detective side of the RIC. These were the beginnings of the so-called 'Dublin Castle Scandals', to which veiled references appear in many memoirs of the period. The editor of the paper, the energetic William O'Brien, was sued by Gustavus Cornwall, the secretary of the General Post Office, and by George Bolton, the Crown Solicitor, who he suggested was guilty of legal malfeasance. French did not dare to sue. The evidence given during the civil cases, which O'Brien won, led to criminal charges. It was alleged that French used his office to suborn young men under his command for homosexual acts. The jury disagreed, but the old man who ran the 'disorderly house' at 43 Golden Lane off Ship Street, just to the rear of the Castle, was jailed. As the contemporary song had, 'it's the rich what gets the pleasure, and the poor as gets the blame'. The culprits disappeared from Ireland, and in the following year French was made bankrupt by the doctor who had claimed in court he was insane.

In Catholic Ireland, criminal acts of sodomy by a government officer with his subordinates could only be frowned upon; and indeed would have been shocking elsewhere as well. The judge in one of the cases remarked upon the '*evidence of a most horrible and repulsive character and offensive to every sense of morality and decency*'. French, according to the Dublin street wit of the day, had been caught '*interfering with Her Majesty's males*'.

The political value of this to nationalists of all kinds was that it cast a taint over the officials who administered British rule in Ireland. But Dublin Castle remained implacable. With the passing of the Franchise Act in 1884 Ireland was moving towards a wider democracy. But the administration was not responsible to this franchise, but to London. Joseph Chamberlain was hardly exaggerating in 1885 when he claimed that the majority of English people had no idea of the system at work in Ireland, a system reinforced by armed power. Just as it had been earlier in the century, it was a completely centralised system akin to that with which Russia governed Poland.

'An Irishman at this moment cannot move a step; he cannot lift a finger in any parochial, municipal, or educational work, without being confronted with, interfered with, controlled by an English official, appointed by a foreign government, and without a shade or shadow of representative authority. I say the time has come to reform the absurd and irritating anachronism known as Dublin Castle.'

By now Parnell was in his stride as leader of the Irish party. Land Acts had been secured, a Home Rule Bill had been introduced in 1887 and, though it had been defeated, it was a movement forward. The return of Lord Salisbury later the same year also saw a return of stiffer measures, the defeat of Parnell's Tenants' Relief Bill, and the beginning of the plan of campaign, and yet another Crimes Bill. The long period of Conservative administration witnessed renewed campaigns against Parnell by *The Times* of London. They claimed, on the basis of letters supposedly signed by Parnell, that he had been involved with the Invincibles and had counselled the Phoenix Park Murders. This charge led on to the Parnell Commission, the exposure of Pigott as the forger of the letters and, by that dreadful quirk which many suspected had been manipulated by Dublin Castle, the downfall and death of Parnell in 1891. It was truly a hectic period in Irish history.

ABOVE: *Charles Stewart Parnell, from a memorial photograph issued after his death*

ABOVE: *Modern
sculptural form at
night in the Moat
Pool – a contem-
porary aspect of an
ancient building*
DUBLIN CASTLE

*The inauguration
ceremony of Mary
Robinson as
President of Ireland,
3 December 1990 –
one of the grand
state occasions for
which St Patrick's
Hall is used*

The Irish Times

RIGHT: *The mixed architectural history of the Castle*

BELOW: *The south range of the Castle*

ABOVE: *The Irish Volunteers saluting the Statue of William III in College Green, painting by Francis Wheatley.*

NATIONAL GALLERY OF IRELAND

RIGHT: *Irish soldiers with axes*

SIR JOHN GILBERT, FACSIMILES OF THE NATIONAL MANUSCRIPTS OF IRELAND, 1878

LEFT: *Norman knights who sometimes espoused the ideals of chivalry*

SIR JOHN GILBERT, FACSIMILES OF THE NATIONAL MANUSCRIPTS OF IRELAND, 1878

BELOW: *St Patrick's Hall, in which the banners of the Knights of St Patrick still hang*

AN DÚCHAS THE HERITAGE SERVICE

LEFT: *The Wardobe Tower, later Records Tower*

LEFT: *The Chester Beatty Library and Oriental Gallery*

BELOW: *Hibernia and the wounded Irish soldier of the Boer War Campaign, one of the surviving fragments of John Hughes' famous memorial to Queen Victoria in the roof garden of the Castle*

93

OPPOSITE, TOP: *The Kane Room, one of the new reception rooms in the Coach House*

DUBLIN CASTLE

OPPOSITE, BOTTOM: *Conference room in the new Castle facilities*

DUBLIN CASTLE

LEFT: *Staircase on the new centre*

DUBLIN CASTLE

RIGHT: *Dining room for delegates*

DUBLIN CASTLE

ABOVE: *Modern media gathering at Dublin Castle, now the scene of constant newsworthy events*
DUBLIN CASTLE

LEFT: *Old and new fabric in the Castle today*
DUBLIN CASTLE

*The Upper Castle
Yard, as it was
during the last
Royal visits to
Ireland*

Lawrence Collection,
National Library of
Ireland

ABOVE: *The Banqueting Hall (otherwise the Picture Gallery)*

LAWRENCE COLLECTION, NATIONAL LIBRARY OF IRELAND

ABOVE: *The Picture Gallery, when not used for state dinners*

LAWRENCE COLLECTION, NATIONAL LIBRARY OF IRELAND

RIGHT: *The State Drawing Room in Victorian days*

LAWRENCE COLLECTION, NATIONAL LIBRARY OF IRELAND

ABOVE: *The Throne Room, with the throne said to have been cut down to fit the diminutive figure of Queen Victoria*

LAWRENCE COLLECTION, NATIONAL LIBRARY OF IRELAND

LEFT: *The State Corridor off which were the State Bedrooms, where Royal guests stayed*

LAWRENCE COLLECTION, NATIONAL LIBRARY OF IRELAND

ABOVE: *St Patrick's Hall arranged for a reception with seats for the Viceroy and his consort*

LAWRENCE COLLECTION, NATIONAL LIBRARY OF IRELAND

THE SOCIAL HEYDAY OF THE CASTLE

In *Muslin*, his novel about Irish society originally published as *A Drama in Muslin* in June 1886, George Moore placed his story in the Castle Season of 1882, so that the Land League troubles and the Phoenix Park murders would make a sombre background to his delineation of the Dublin marriage market.

Moore himself, however, was not in Dublin that season, though he was a frequent visitor to the family estate which he owned in Mayo. His Dublin visit was made for the Season of 1886, and produced not only the novel but also a series of articles for *Le Figaro*, published in Paris that summer, which he later collected as *Terre d'Irlande (Parnell and His Island)* published in June, 1887.

One of his essays there dealt with Dublin Castle, and the social life that surrounded it in the clubs and grand hotels of the city in the Season. These pieces were written from an original point of view. Moore was the son of a prominent Home Rule parliamentarian, but he did not write as a nationalist. He had been reared as a Catholic, but he was no longer sympathetic to the Church. He wrote as a worldly, indeed pagan, poet returned from Paris, with rumours of dark sins hovering about his head, which he nevertheless reconciled with his social status as a landlord in his own right.

In January 1884 he arrived in Dublin from the west of Ireland to savour the Season as material for his new novel. At this time he was enamoured of a young lady called Miss Maud Browne, but the girl in his novel also had other models. When he arrived in Dublin his first concern was to buy the proper clothes. A complete Court suit cost £45, but he managed to borrow all he needed except for the very formal velvets. He saved £25 and at the end of the season sold the velvets for £10. He stayed at the Shelbourne Hotel (like Mr Harding, his alter ego in the novel), where he worked on the novel in the mornings before the social round of the evening.

He failed to marry Maude, but the régime to which she was subjected by her family suggested the theme of *Muslin*.

I have been to a state ball at the Castle [he wrote to his mother on 17 February 1884], *and I have to confess that I found it very grand and imposing. The Catholic lot I know by heart, and as I considered them low, commonplace and uneducated, I avoided them. At the State ball I did not stir from the end of the room near the dais where I danced a few times with Lady Bellew, a young lady she was chaperoning, Miss Dease, the chamberlain's daughter, Miss Burke, Lady Fingal's sister and Miss Butler. There was a Calico ball given at the Rotunda. Never did I see anything so low, vile, so dirty. Dublin society has lost all sense of what is la vie comme il faut. Men blacking their faces to go and dance with the ladies – it was awful.*

These events – the Levée, State Ball, and Calico Ball – would all find a place at the heart of his projected novel. His biographer Joseph Hone found in the 1930s that '*certain old ladies, debutantes of that season, still remember dancing with him. "My recollection," one of them says, "is a red-faced affable young man, excellent company, but of a sudden and uncertain temper. One never knew when or why he would become ruffled or bored, or annoyed with you."'*

Moore returned to Mayo to write the draft of his novel and articles in the winter of 1884-5. But he found

OPPOSITE:

Fashionable ladies walking in the Pound during the Castle social season

THE GRAPHIC, COURTESY MONT CLARE HOTEL

then that there was one thing he had missed, as he explained in a letter to Colonel Dease (18 January 1885):

I am actively engaged on a book, in the interests of which I came to Dublin last year to attend the Levée, the Drawing Rooms and the Castle Balls. I was not fortunate enough to receive an invitation for a State dinner party. Now, as my book deals with the social and political power of the Castle in modern Ireland, I should be glad to attend the Levée in February [1885], if I could be sure of being asked to one of the big dinner parties. My books, as you are probably aware, are extensively read; this particular one will attract a great deal of attention. It would be therefore well to render my picture as complete, as true, as vivid as possible.

It is likely that, though a prominent landlord, the reputation of Moore as the author of *A Modern Lover* and *A Mummer's Wife* would have gone before him to the State Steward. It may well be, as Hone suggests, that in his simplicity Moore thought the Viceroy and the Castle would be only too delighted to be turned into a Zolaesque novel. But then, realising his error, he began to bombard the Castle with notes by messenger and when at last they replied that 'the lists are at present closed', Moore took the whole correspondence to the *Freeman's Journal*, the leading nationalist paper of the day, which was already sniping at Lord Spencer's coercive administration.

For the time being he became something of a hero among nationalist MPs, and the affair was also reported in the British press. These adventures of George Moore's were also recalled by Daisy Burke, later Daisy Fingal, in her own delightful memoirs.

* * *

Also in 1885, on 9 August, the Prince of Wales, on one of those rare Victorian royal visits to Ireland, held a Levée at Dublin Castle. The Princess of Wales held a Drawing Room at the Castle. Their business in the city was to lay the foundation stone of the Science and Art Museum (the core of the present National Museum and National Library). This event was an indication of changes in Ireland that had little to do with

political matters – social and technical changes that would create new conditions requiring new responses. It was those responses that failed. For one of the changes was the rise, marked at the election that year, of Orange opinion in Ulster, which from this date effectively cut off the industrialised north-east from the rest of the island.

* * *

On Wednesday the Lord Lieutenant gave a large ball at the Castle to the servants of the Viceregal Court and their friends. The ball was opened by the Countess of Aberdeen and this was probably the first instance of a Lady Lieutenant descending from the pedestal of her dignity to inaugurate the amusements of her dependants.

Court Society Review, March 1886

* * *

Lord Aberdeen had arrived in February 1886 but lasted as Viceroy only until August. More significant was the arrival of Arthur Balfour as Chief Secretary in March 1887. That year saw the celebration in Dublin of the Jubilee of the Queen's accession to the throne.

The Diamond Jubilee in 1896 was marked in Dublin by yet another royal visit by the Duke and Duchess of York, who arrived on 18 August. The next day the Duke received addresses from the Throne Room at the Castle, and after that took the oath as a member of the Privy Council for Ireland. The Duke and the Irish-born Field Marshal Lord Roberts ('Bobs' of Kandahar fame) were invested as Knights of St Patrick. The royal couple then departed on a tour of Ireland.

This royal enthusiasm in Dublin was balanced of course by other events, such as the celebration of the Rising of 1798 and the laying of a foundation stone of a statue to Wolfe Tone in St Stephen's Green.

Royal visits had been made, as we have seen, in the early part of Victoria's reign, but the Widow of Windsor was not concerned to appear in public. She did come again in 1900, shortly before her death, to mark her appreciation of the part played by the Irish in fighting the Boers in South Africa. Though much is heard these days about the 150 or so soldiers who fought with Major MacBride's Irish brigade in South Africa, they were as nothing compared with the 58,000 who served with the regular British regiments.

The Queen made her state entry into Dublin on 4 April 1900. At Leeson Street Bridge, where temporary city gates in lath and plaster had been erected, the Lord Mayor presented an address of welcome. (Some would have noted that the royal progress was halted before the door of Davy's Tavern in Upper Leeson St, in which the Invincibles had celebrated their victory in May 1882.)

The next day there was a grand parade of troops in Phoenix Park, and as a memento of her visit the Queen presented the city with a silver mether (an ancient Celtic drinking cup). She left on 23 April. Nine months later she was dead, and Edward VII was proclaimed King. The King made his first visit to Dublin in 1903. The Queen presented badges to Jubilee Nurses in St Patrick's Hall, and then they held a Levée, afterwards visiting Trinity College Dublin. A military review was also held and the King and Queen held Court in Dublin Castle. Among the various visits,

mostly to hospitals and charities, they also visited Maynooth where they were presented with a loyal address by the assembled clerics of the Catholic Church. After a week's tour of the country through Belfast, Derry, Galway, and Cork, they left from Kingstown on 1 August. Though the king at his departure issued a gracious message 'To My Irish People', the controversy in Dublin Corporation over the presentation of a Loyal Address was more indicative of what the real trend of feeling had been ever since the fall of Parnell in 1891. In the city, forces to bring down the Empire were gathering momentum.

BELOW: *The Upper Castle Yard during the social season in the 1870s*

RIGHT: *The former Detective Office in Exchange Court, outside which detective Patrick Synnott died, and inside which Volunteers Clancy and McKee and Conor Clune were murdered*

CHAPTER ELEVEN

THE LAST DAYS OF THE EMPIRE

On 24 December 1892 a violent explosion wrecked the Dublin detective office in Exchange Court, killing a policeman named Patrick Synnott, who was returning to the mess after some time away in hospital.

This was one of a series of explosions in Dublin which seem to have been the work of a group angered at the government's refusal to release the Clan na Gael members, who had bombed London a decade before, and the last of the Invincibles. Among the first people on the scene was Inspector Mallon, who rushed there from his house in the Lower Castle Yard. The unfortunate policeman had his legs blown off, a boot landing over the top of the house in the Lower Yard. Other bombs were later thrown into the Four Courts and Aldborough barracks. These bombs, coming so soon after the death of Parnell, were a last gesture of 'the old guard', but it failed to move the Castle administration.

The Castle was the centre of a great web reaching out through policemen and informers to every corner of the country. In 1904, during the anti-semitic eruptions in Limerick, the Chief Secretary was able to respond to a strong protest from the Chief Rabbi of England with an inquiry that established within days that the myths about Jewish pedlars having farming communities in deep hock were just that – myths.

Towards the end of the century the Castle saw many changes. This was the beginning of what a recent writer, Laurence W. McBride, characterised as 'the greening of Dublin Castle', the process by which the English staff was slowly replaced by competent Irishmen, often of a national, though not always a nationalist, bent. This was a reaction to the inevitable arrival of Home Rule perhaps, but it meant that when Ireland achieved its independence it had in place a Civil Service which smoothed the transition from colony to country. But the upper ranks remained filled from London.

Some mourned the slow passing of the old system. The term of Earl Cadogan (1895–1900), according to Thomas Sadleir, '*marks the last of the great Viceroys, though there was a good deal of entertaining during that of Lord Dudley*'. William Humble War, Earl of Dudley, is '*the lord lieutenant general and general governor of Ireland*' (1902–06) whose progress through the city is one of the set-pieces of James Joyce's *Ulysses*, on that memorable day, 16 June 1904, with all the varied reactions of the very varied citizens:

The cavalcade passed by the lower gate of Phoenix park saluted by obsequious policemen and proceeded past Kingsbridge along the northern quays ... From its sluice in Wood quay under Tom Devan's office Poddle river hung out in fealty a tongue of liquid sewage. Above the crossblind of the Ormond Hotel, gold by bronze, Miss Kennedy's head by Miss Douce's head watched and admired. On Ormond quay Mr Simon Dedalus, steering his way from the greenhouse for the subsheriff's office, stood still in the street and brought his hat low.

Sadleir's remark about the decline of viceregal entertaining was affected perhaps by his connection with the Office of Arms. In the popular view, that of the man in the street such as Simon Dedalus, the most significant of the later Viceroys were undoubtedly the Aberdeens, though they were not much liked in some official circles.

FAR RIGHT: *Lady Aberdeen; and* RIGHT: *Lord Aberdeen*

Their ideas of whom to entertain were very different.

On 3 February 1906, the Aberdeens made their state entry into Dublin, returning some twenty years after their great success between 1886 and 1892. They were among the handful of Viceroys and their wives who had been sympathetic to the nation as a whole, and not to just that part of it that had all too often constituted Castle society. Lady Aberdeen, for instance, was deeply involved in anti-tuberculosis campaigns which were to make her a household name throughout Ireland.

They might have been boycotted by Unionists, but the King made it known that those who avoided the Court in Dublin would not be welcome at the Court of St James. But Ireland had changed. Though the reunited Parliamentary Party was still working for home rule, the rise of Sinn Féin and the Gaelic League had brought new names and new ideals into political life. But though the Aberdeens were as popular as they had ever been, the time was passing when this would be enough. Their very popularity meant that they were disliked in Dublin Castle, and it was Dublin Castle, through the Chief Secretary and the Under Secretary, that ran Ireland.

The Aberdeens were to remain until 1915, and were followed by three more Viceroys. But already history was closing in. Through the ranks of many Irish organisations the hand of the IRB was operating secretly, creating the circumstances when it could revolt. Many who with the best will in the world threw themselves into working for Ireland would have been dismayed to learn how conspirators, working much as the Communists and Trotskyists would later work, were suborning their legal and constitutional efforts to revolutionary ends. But all this was behind the scenes; the daily drama was of a more comic genre.

THE THEFT OF THE IRISH CROWN JEWELS

In July, 1907, the thrilling news went out that the Crown Jewels in Dublin Castle were missing. In Charles II's reign an Irishman named Blood stole the English regalia; now we have an unknown man stealing royal jewels in Dublin Castle. Valued at £50,000, these were in the custody of Sir Arthur Vicars, the Ulster King of Arms; but despite the combined efforts of all Europe's detectives, and the holding of a sworn inquiry into the circumstances, mystery surrounds their disappearance to this day. Fortunately, some of the larger articles were not stolen; the great Sword of State and the massive silver-gilt maces remaining safely in the strong room of the Office of Arms.

The story, however, does not end there. Sir Arthur Vicars refused to hand over to his successor the keys of the strong room till the very day before the arrival of King Edward VII in Dublin, when the remaining pieces of the regalia would have to be produced. Then, flinging the precious bunch of keys through the bars of the steel grille, Sir Arthur banged the outer door and went away. Here was a pretty problem. The keys were far in the room, the door securely locked, with no possible way to get in save by breaking through the thick wall of steel and concrete, and only a few hours to do it. Workmen were employed with an oxy-hydrogen flame to eat through the steel; even burglars, it was rumoured, were called out of the Dublin gaols to assist. The night wore on. A hole a few inches wide had been made when the experts announced that it would be impossible to enlarge it sufficiently to admit a man within the necessary time. A slow task it had been, for the story got abroad that the gas-jets in the strong room had been left on, so that when an aperture was made it was feared there would be a terrific explosion. All present felt that a calamity was impending, for it was known that Edward VII would be much annoyed if the State Sword and Maces – those emblems of the King's authority – could not be produced on his arrival.

'I have it,' suddenly shouted a stalwart policeman standing by, 'Get the smallest thing that can walk, and push it through the hole!' This idea was at once acted upon; the slums adjoining the Castle being scoured by the police for a small child. But to expect any Irishwoman, a little after midnight, to lend her baby to an enormous policeman who wished to take him to the Castle proved a difficult matter. It was only by much wheedling that a puny mite was procured. He, too, sobbed so bitterly that it was necessary to knock up a sweet-shop, and indulge the babe with a plentiful supply of a confection known as Peggy's Leg, before he would go quietly to the Castle, where, after being with difficulty pushed into the strong room, the little fellow retrieved the missing keys.

from The Romance of Dublin Castle
by Thomas Ulick Sadleir

The theft of the Crown Jewels in 1907 from the Chief Herald's office, on the eve of a Royal visit to Ireland, focused attention on the Office of Arms. 'Ireland is not a joke,' Mr Birrell had said. 'Certainly not,' replied the journalist, R. Barry O'Brien, but assuredly the Office of Arms was a joke. In 1903 it had moved from the Record Tower to the Bedford Tower, where Sir Arthur

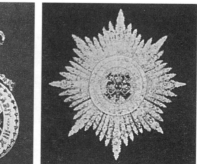

BELOW LEFT: *The Irish Crown Jewels stolen from the Bedford Tower in 1907*

ABOVE: *Sir Arthur Vicars in his Herald's tabard*
GENEALOGICAL OFFICE

Vicars had continued to build up the museum and archive begun by the Burkes. Sir John Burke (1815–92) had been the son of Tipperary-born John Burke (1787–1848), who had founded Burke's Peerage in 1826. Sir John was appointed Ulster-King-at-Arms in succession to Sir John Betham in 1853. He founded the series Burke's *Landed Gentry of Ireland*, through which

RIGHT: *Queen
Alexandra,
photographed in
Dublin*

BELOW RIGHT:
*Gentlemen in
Court Dress on
their way into a
Levée*
MICHAL TULLY, OLD
DUBLIN SOCIETY

can be traced what Michael Davitt called 'the fall of feudal Ireland', and which has now become Burke's *Family Records*. To this set of scholars modern researchers are deeply indebted for their years of work in epitomising records now lost to us. But to a certain kind of modern mind, impatient for improvement, poring over the fragmentary records of the past was a waste of time – and money. The total expenditure on the Office of Arms for the year 1906–7 was about £900, with salaries ranging from £500 for Ulster, Sir Arthur Vicars, down to £5 for the occasional coal porter.

The robbery, however, was not a joke but quickly became a scandal, and remains to this day a mystery which has never quite been resolved. Vicars, excitable and effeminate, was suspected of being part of a homosexual set in Dublin Castle circles. It was thought he had been drugged at home by one of his set,

and his keys removed and copied. This rumour certainly added a further level of sensation to the story.

After an inquiry Vicars resigned, having been made the scapegoat for the failure of security. He was murdered by men posing as the IRA in 1921 on the front lawn of his Kerry home. To the end he had no doubts about who was responsible. He named the culprit in his will, dated 14 May 1920, but the High Court and the Deputy Keeper of the Records sealed this passage from public view until a recent date. (The Irish government referred to is, of course, the British administration of the day.)

I might have had more to dispose of had it not been for the outrageous way in which I was treated by the Irish Govt. over the loss of the Irish Crown Jewels in 1907, backed up by the late King Edward VII whom I had always loyally and faithfully served, when I was made a scape goat to save other departments responsible and when they shielded the real culprit and thief, Francis R, Shackleton (brother of the explorer who did not reach the South Pole). My whole life and work was ruined by this cruel misfortune and by the wicked and blackguardly acts of the Irish government. I had sunk my whole fortune in my profession and was left without any means but for the magnanimous conduct of my dear brother George Gun Mahony. I am unconscious of having done anyone any wrong and my misfortune arose from by being unsuspicious and trusting a one-time friend and the official of my former office. I had hoped to leave a legacy to my dear little dog 'Romie' had he not been taken from me this year. Well we shall meet in 'the next world'.

Dublin Castle survived the scandal. However, after Vicars resigned, Captain (later Sir) Neville Wilkinson, a Guards officer, replaced him as a safe pair

of hands. Wilkinson is still remembered by the older generation as the creator of the famous doll's house, Titania's Palace, which he used to raise funds for children's charities, and he made many improvements, leading to the eventual opening of an Heraldic Museum by the Lord Lieutenant on 20 April 1909.

This museum still exists, and is still added to, though it has now been removed from the Bedford Tower to the National Library in Kildare Street, where the Chief Heralds now have their offices. On the wall of the corridor there hangs a portrait in pastels of Sir Arthur Vicars in his Herald's uniform.

R. Barry O'Brien, the journalist quoted in Sadleir above, who was Parnell's first biographer, spent several months in Dublin in 1907 investigating the workings of the British administration, which he published as *Dublin Castle and the Irish People*. (A new edition of this book appeared in March 1912 at the time of the final Home Rule Bill.) '*The case of the Irish people is the right to make their own laws in their own Parliament on their own soil.*' Though, like many nationalists, O'Brien played down the internal divisions of Ireland herself, what he described was a complete machinery of government, with a full range of departments and boards all located in Ireland and staffed largely by Irishmen, but which was controlled by an official answerable not to the Irish people but to the English Cabinet. If Home Rule came, what would happen to Dublin Castle? he asked in conclusion.

'The Castle would remain where it is, but not what it is. Some Englishmen think that by the abolition of the Castle all that is wrong in the Administration would be set right. Not at all.

'The objections are to the English character of the Castle. Make it Irish and the objections will disappear. It can be made Irish by becoming a centre of government based on the popular will. Such a Government means National Autonomy ... The Irish people do not want the abolition of Dublin Castle in order to put the Home Office or Downing Street, or both, in its place. The stream of Irish Administration is corrupt; but the poison flows from the sources and is not generated by any of the tributaries. The source is on the English side of the Channel. A Governor practically chosen by the Irish people, though nominated by the Common Sovereign; a Parliament representing the Irish people; and an Executive (Dublin Castle) under the influence of public opinion – these are the terms which

LEFT: *King Edward VII, photographed in Dublin*

BELOW LEFT:
Debutantes being presented to Lord and Lady Aberdeen at the Viceregal Court

the present generation of Irishmen are prepared to accept in settlement of the account; though it is only the expression of political wisdom to add, in the words of Parnell, 'no man has the right to fix the boundary of the march of a nation.'

It was clear that Home Rule in some form was on its way. As part of the conciliation process there were more royal visits. Queen Victoria had made two visits in the lifetime of Prince Albert and, as the Widow of Windsor, had travelled to Dublin in April 1900 to thank her Irish subjects for their contribution to the Boer War. King Edward VII had come in 1903 and 1904, the Prince of Wales in 1905, the King and Queen again in 1907. King George V in his turn came to Ireland in 1911 for a five-day visit, the high points of which were the opening of the new premises of the Royal College of Science (today the home of the Irish government) and a visit to Maynooth. There was an address at Dublin Castle on 10 July, followed by a Levée. A state banquet was followed by a Chapter of the Order of St Patrick, when the Earl of Shaftesbury and Viscount Kitchener were invested as Extra Knights. Their majesties left Ireland for Holyhead on 12 July; on 1 October John Redmond unveiled the statue of Parnell at the junction of O'Connell Street and Great Britain Street, which was now renamed Parnell Street. The King and John Redmond were living in different Irelands.

With the labour disturbances of 1913, the resistance to Home Rule in Ulster and the founding of the

RIGHT: *James Larkin, from a sketch made in August 1923 by Sir William Orpen*

Irish Volunteers, the view from Dublin Castle was becoming a disturbing one. During August and September the great Dublin Lock-Out disturbed the city. In October 1913 a Board of Trade inquiry under Sir George Askwith sat in Dublin Castle to hear evidence from both sides. Among the witnesses called to the Castle was Jim Larkin, who denounced the employers in no uncertain terms.

The rhetoric of Revolution had come to the Castle. Soon the Revolution followed.

From an address to the Board of Trade Court of Inquiry chaired by Sir George Askwith, Dublin Castle, 5 October 1913
Having referred to the housing conditions and the poverty in 'this Catholic City of Dublin, the most church-going city, I believe, in the world', Larkin declared: The workers are determined that this state of affairs must cease. Christ will not be crucified in Dublin by these men.

This Lock-Out will arouse a social conscience in Dublin and in Ireland generally. I am out to help to arouse that social conscience and to lift up better the lot of those who are sweated and exploited.

The Irish workmen are out to get access to the means of life. They are not going to be slaves; they are not going to allow their women to be slaves of a brutal capitalistic system which has neither a soul to be saved nor a soft place to be kicked.

I am engaged in holy work. I have worked hard from an early age. I made the best of my opportunities. I have been called anti-Christ. I have been called an atheist. Well, if I were an atheist I would not deny it. I am a Socialist.

When I came to Dublin I found that the men on the quays had been paid their wages in public houses, and if they did not waste most of their money there, they would not get work the next time. Every stevedore was getting ten per cent of the money taken by the publican from the worker, and the man who would not spend his money across the counter was not wanted.

I have tried to lift men up out of the state of degradation. No monetary benefit has accrued to me. I have taken up the task through intense love of my class. I have given the men a stimulus, heart and hope which they never had before. I have made men out of drunken gaol-birds.

Is it any wonder a Larkin arose? Was there not a need for a Larkin? If the employers want peace they can have peace, but if they want war they will get war.

This great fight of ours is not simply a question of shorter hours or better wages. It is a great fight for human liberty, liberty to live as human beings should live, exercising their God-given faculties and powers over nature; always aiming to reach out for a higher betterment and development, trying to achieve in our own time the dreams of great thinkers and poets of this nation not as some men do, working for their own individual betterment and aggrandisement

POBLACHT NA H EIREANN.
THE PROVISIONAL GOVERNMENT
OF THE
IRISH REPUBLIC
TO THE PEOPLE OF IRELAND.

IRISHMEN AND IRISHWOMEN: In the name of God and of the dead generations from which she receives her old tradition of nationhood, Ireland, through us, summons her children to her flag and strikes for her freedom.

Having organised and trained her manhood through her secret revolutionary organisation, the Irish Republican Brotherhood, and through her open military organisations, the Irish Volunteers and the Irish Citizen Army, having patiently perfected her discipline, having resolutely waited for the right moment to reveal itself, she now seizes that moment, and, supported by her exiled children in America and by gallant allies in Europe, but relying in the first on her own strength, she strikes in full confidence of victory.

We declare the right of the people of Ireland to the ownership of Ireland, and to the unfettered control of Irish destinies, to be sovereign and indefeasible. The long usurpation of that right by a foreign people and government has not extinguished the right, nor can it ever be extinguished except by the destruction of the Irish people. In every generation the Irish people have asserted their right to national freedom and sovereignty; six times during the past three hundred years they have asserted it in arms. Standing on that fundamental right and again asserting it in arms in the face of the world, we hereby proclaim the Irish Republic as a Sovereign Independent State, and we pledge our lives and the lives of our comrades-in-arms to the cause of its freedom, of its welfare, and of its exaltation among the nations.

The Irish Republic is entitled to, and hereby claims, the allegiance of every Irishman and Irishwoman. The Republic guarantees religious and civil liberty, equal rights and equal opportunities to all its citizens, and declares its resolve to pursue the happiness and prosperity of the whole nation and of all its parts, cherishing all the children of the nation equally, and oblivious of the differences carefully fostered by an alien government, which have divided a minority from the majority in the past.

Until our arms have brought the opportune moment for the establishment of a permanent National Government, representative of the whole people of Ireland and elected by the suffrages of all her men and women, the Provisional Government, hereby constituted, will administer the civil and military affairs of the Republic in trust for the people.

We place the cause of the Irish Republic under the protection of the Most High God, Whose blessing we invoke upon our arms, and we pray that no one who serves that cause will dishonour it by cowardice, inhumanity, or rapine. In this supreme hour the Irish nation must, by its valour and discipline and by the readiness of its children to sacrifice themselves for the common good, prove itself worthy of the august destiny to which it is called.

Signed on Behalf of the Provisional Government,

THOMAS J. CLARKE,

SEAN Mac DIARMADA,   THOMAS MacDONAGH,
P. H. PEARSE,   EAMONN CEANNT,
JAMES CONNOLLY.   JOSEPH PLUNKETT.

RIGHT: *The 1916 Proclamation of the Irish Republic, the founding document of modern Ireland*

CHAPTER TWELVE

RESURGENT IRELAND

The story of Ireland's road to freedom has often been told, but almost always from an Irish point of view. From the perspective of the Imperial executive in Dublin Castle, which Barry O'Brien and his kind had excoriated, it had often seemed that the empire might yet be saved from Irish 'disloyalty'. Hundreds of thousands of Irishmen rallied to the flag in the Great War, but at home a handful of revolutionaries would change the course of history.

When the Great War broke out in August 1914, during Lord Aberdeen's final term of office, the usual festivities at Dublin Castle were suspended for the duration. Under his successor, Lord Wimborne, the grand rooms of the State Apartments were fitted up as a military hospital run by the Red Cross, where soldiers from the Western Front could recuperate.

In the months before the Easter Rising in April 1916, the Irish Citizen Army under James Connolly had made practice feints at attacking the Castle. However, these were not taken seriously by the authorities, even though it was later rumoured that Connolly had rejected a proposal to burn down the Castle because of the Red Cross hospital there. The leading figure in the Red Cross fund-raising for this Hospital was none other than

RIGHT: *The main gate of Dublin Castle with the Guard House outside which the policeman was shot dead on Easter Monday*

LAWRENCE COLLECTION, NATIONAL LIBRARY OF IRELAND

William Martin Murphy (whose paper the *Irish Independent* would later call in an editorial for Connolly's execution).

Two views exist, one provided by Sir Matthew Nathan from the top; and the other by a nurse in the Red Cross Hospital from the bottom.

* * *

The Irish Times, which was Unionist in its sympathies, reported the last assault on the Castle.

About noon on Easter Monday a party of armed Volunteers and men of the Citizen Army entered the precincts of Dublin Castle. A policeman at the Upper Castle Gate was shot dead, and some of the men scaled the gates. At the same time armed men forced their way into the City Hall, and got out on the roof, when they commanded the main entrance to the Castle. They also took possession of the Dublin Daily Express newspaper office, and from the roof and windows they guarded the approaches – Dame Street, Castle Street and Cork Hill – to the Upper Castle Yard ... Intermittent firing continued around the Castle practically all day on Easter Monday. The regular troops, it was reported, regained possession of the Upper Yard in the afternoon, but skirmishes and free firing went on around the Castle until a late hour that night.

RIGHT: *Dave Neligan, 'The Spy in the Castle'*
CENTRAL CATHOLIC LIBRARY

One of those killed in the attack on the City Hall was Sean Connolly, of the Abbey Theatre, who had appeared with the Countess Markievicz in the patriotic play about revolutionaries, *The Memory of the Dead.*

On Thursday of Easter Week James Connolly was slightly wounded in one arm. This wound was dressed by Dr Jim Ryan, but later in the day Connolly was carried into the hospital with a severe wound in his ankle. He was given chloroform to kill the pain and the leg was put in splints. He was later taken back into the main hall of the GPO, where he continued to direct operations from a bed. After the Rising James Connolly was taken to the hospital in Dublin Castle, where he was placed in a separate guarded room. (The room which is today shown to visitors as that in which he was detained is in fact one of the rooms totally reconstructed in the 1960s, and not the original.)

* * *

However, the Rising was merely a prelude to the real fighting, which began in 1919. During the Troubles Dublin Castle was at the very storm-centre of the swirling political passions.

The much vaunted intelligence system of the Castle seems in effect not to have been so powerful as legend had rumoured it. David Neligan (later an officer in the Guards with a house in the Castle) then worked in the Dublin Metropolitan Police. He had resigned from the police, but was persuaded by Michael Collins to rejoin and to serve as his 'spy in the Castle'. On one occasion Neligan smuggled Collins into the Castle, where, undetected, he passed the night scanning the secret files of the administration.

Neligan's perspectives on the last days of British

rule are revealing. But even more revealing is his reluctance to speak about the Civil War or about later events such as his dismissal from the Guards in 1932 with the advent of de Valera.

The Dublin Metropolitan Police area was divided into Divisions A, B, C, D, E and F. The detective division was therefore known as G. The British Government in Ireland organised the G-men at the time of the Fenians [1865–67] to combat that body. Members were drawn from the uniformed force and they served their British masters well. After the collapse of the 1916 rising, the G-men picked out the leaders for court martial and deportation. This excited the wrath of Michael Collins, who on his release from prison started to reorganise both the I.R.B. and the I.R.A. The G-men got ready to resume their espionage but several were summarily shot and those responsible escaped arrest. Also, Collins organised sympathisers in their ranks and turned the machine against itself. This was a body-blow for the British and one from which they did not recover.

Collins had four informants inside the Castle, who included, apart from Neligan, Ned Broy and a cousin, who was surprised when she was given special responsibility of ensuring that papers did not pass into the hands of the IRA. Collins was astonished. 'In the name of God how did these people ever get an empire?'

It was during the Troubles that three volunteers were actually murdered in the police office in Exchange Court. In the early hours of Sunday, 21 November 1920, Dick McKee (Commandant of the Dublin Brigade IRA), Peadar Clancy (Vice-Commandant and Director of Munitions) and Conor Clune were arrested in a raid on a house in Lower Gloucester Street, and brought to the Dublin Castle police office in Exchange Court. In the guardroom a little later all three were shot. A Court of Inquiry found that the Auxiliary Division RIC had killed them in 'self-defence' and in pursuit of their duty to prevent them from escaping. All three had been tortured, as the condition of the bodies later released to their families showed. Still before dawn on the same day, Michael Collins' men murdered fourteen British intelligence officers, while in the afternoon the British killed twelve and wounded sixty people at a match in Croke Park. Collins had been supplied with annotated photographs, one at least taken in the Upper Castle Yard which showed the officers in plain clothes. This was the weekend of 'Bloody Sunday'.

Though the old police building is now no longer public property and the little room once preserved as a memorial to the three men has been done away with, a plaque on the exterior wall of this oddly insignificant yet sinister building marks this grim event. The room itself is no longer on the visitors' itinerary.

After Bloody Sunday, officers (and their wives) were made to live in the Castle itself, as were civil servants brought from England and other intelligence men. Charles Bewley, later a Free State ambassador in Berlin and the Vatican, describes in his memoirs the siege atmosphere of the Castle while he was acting as a defence lawyer for Republicans being tried in the temporary court established in the City Hall, all the buildings being surrounded by barricades of barbed wire and armed guards.

Despite the imposition of these draconian measures, the war was lost. Home Rule had, after all, been granted in 1914 – British public opinion was resigned to the 'loss' of at least part of Ireland. A truce was reached in July 1921, and on 6 August Dublin Castle ordered the release of the detained deputies of the Second Dáil. The road to the Treaty (6 December 1921) and to the Civil War had opened.

* * *

The Castle regime was notorious for its nourishment of informers through the ages and paid out millions to them. I do not suppose that informers are popular anywhere, but a terrible odium attached to them in Ireland, where memories are long indeed. At one time the Castle maintained a home for them in Dublin to save their lives. In my presence an old policeman said of a colleague: 'Sure he couldn't be good, his great-grandfather was reared in the informers' home!'

from *A Spy in the Castle* (1968) by David Neligan

* * *

A Nurse in Dublin Castle

It was shortly after noon on Easter Monday, April 24. I was washing bandages in the Supper Room Kitchen, when a man came in, and, as I thought, said. 'Come quick and look. There is a fire in the Castle.' I went into the Anteroom and looked out of the window, but as I saw nothing of interest, returned to my bandages. In a few minutes he came back. 'You must come and look! They are firing on the Castle!' The Anteroom is really the drawing-room of the Controller's house, and is on the left side of the Square, facing the Lower Yard, and at right angles to the Front Gate, so we could not see much; and as hospital is a place where punctuality reigns supreme, I went back to lay the lockers for the men's dinner.

Then came great excitement. 'The policeman at the Front Gate has been shot, and they have carried him in!' The Sister on our landing was summoned and rushed downstairs, while speculation began as to which policeman it was. It turned out to be the nicest, such a dear, with grey hair and twinkly eyes; he always used to salute us when we passed in uniform, and just grin when we were in mufti.

When the men's dinner was nearly over, Sister came back. She had been helping to tie up the policeman, but there was no hope; death had been instantaneous. She confirmed the rumour that it was our favourite; she said she could just recognise him, though the upper part of his face was destroyed. Then one of the nurses came in, very flushed and excited. She had been off duty for two hours that morning, and had heard rumours of trouble while she was out. On her way back she said to the policeman at the Gate, 'Is it true that the Sinn Feiners are going to take the Castle?' 'No, miss,' he answered, 'the authorities are making much too much fuss about it,' and before she had crossed the Yard and gone in at the door, he had had his brains blown out, and was lying dead on the ground.

The men, who were watching from the windows, said an armed body marched up Cork Hill to the Gate, and shot the policeman through the head. The sentry, who had only blank ammunition, fled into the Guard Room. The Sinn Feiners took the keys and locked the gates.

We heard afterwards that the original plan had been to seize the Castle, as they had done the GPO; and many reasons were advanced why they had not done so. Most people thought it was due to a misunderstanding; that some of the Rebels had gone to a wrong place, and the remaining number were not strong enough. Connolly, however, told us that when they found no resistance, and they thought it must be a trap to entice them in and ambush them, and that Ship Street Barracks, at the back, would be too strong for them. One of the soldiers told me there were only seventy raw recruits in the Barracks, and no ammunition there at the time. I think one of the nurses summed up the situation when she said, 'Somebody was praying for us.'

When the men's dinner was finished and the ward tidied, I ran into the Sterilising Room to see what was happening at the back. A troop of soldiers had arrived, and were drawn up in the Barrack Yard. The heavy solid gates were closed, and also shut across, with a sentry at each peep-hole. Outside, instead of men with bayonets, were a few small children, staring with open mouths at the massive gates! Rifle-shots were heard at intervals, but we could not see where they came from, nor where the bullets went.

At First Dinner there was a general atmosphere of unrest. Conversation flagged, though a few people kept up constant questions — chiefly asking if we had seen the policeman's helmet in the hall, and the holes made by the bullet in it. Suddenly every one jumped up and ran to the window which overlooks the Barrack Yard — but it was only the soldiers drilling. There was a noise of people rushing down the corridor, and the sisters ran out to see if they were needed. Several times during the meal stretchers passed down the corridor outside, and each time we asked the same question: 'Killed or wounded?' and some one came in and said 'Dead' or 'Very bad.'

We could not cross the Yard to our rooms after dinner, so I took a tour through the Picture Gallery and Throne Room, where all windows were thronged with spectators. The Throne Room faces the Front Gate, and from there I could see that the Gate was locked, and guarded by Rebels, I think, in National Volunteer uniform. Otherwise things looked much as usual; men passed up and down Dame Street; only rifle-shots rang out at intervals. 'Look! you can see the sniper; watch the roof of that house,' said one of the men next me. Presently something popped up on the roof – a puff of smoke – bang! I had seen a bullet fired to kill!

When I came back to the Supper Room I found a nurse in great agitation. 'I was nearly killed!' she exclaimed. As there did not seem any immediate danger, I asked how. 'I was leaning out of the Sterilising Room window, and a bullet whizzed right past me – look at the mark on my apron!' She pointed to a rent, which I was convinced had been there all the morning, and tactlessly said so. 'Well, it passed very near me anyway,' she protested, 'and I got such a fright.'

Another officer and a Tommy came up and mixed with the crowd in the Throne Room, so that they could see without being seen. They soon began firing through the window – probably at the sniper I had seen earlier in the afternoon. I was horrified to see the wounded men standing all round; for if the sniper spotted where the shots were coming from, he would no doubt return the compliment. This apparently occurred to the soldiers after-wards, for they turned every one out of the ward, and locked the doors. The firing continued the whole afternoon.

Before the soldiers started firing from the Throne Room window I saw Rebels come into the Yard, look round, and go out again. The men, who were watching, said they unlocked the Gate several times, came in and fired on the Guard Room, and went out again. Rumour said there was a large quantity of ammunition in the Lower Yard, which was their objective. The gates between the Upper and Lower Yard were closed, but although there was no guard the Sinn Feiners showed no inclination to force them.

About 5 p.m. troops arrived. They were lined up in the Yard when I first saw them, so I do not know which gate they came through. We did not know what regiments they were, nor where they had come from. I had to take the temperatures of the men sitting at the windows, which gave me an opportunity to look out; but beyond the lines of troops, nothing of interest seemed to be happening.

Presently there was a stir of expectancy. We all waited breathless, and round the corner came the milkman rolling a big can! He was greeted by cheer upon cheer from the windows, as no one had thought there was any prospect of the evening's milk arriving.

There were a few sentries on guard, their bodies well behind cover, only their eyes peering round to look through the Gate; and any one crossing the Yard had to run across the exposed strip opposite the Front Gate. The first definite movement I noticed among the troops was when an officer and a number of men collected near the Gate; they were lined up, and he gave orders. At a signal he and two or three of the men ran towards the Gate and disappeared from view; three or four followed, and so on. This turned out to be the famous charge on the City Hall.

We had been sent a message: all blinds were to be pulled down and all lights turned out, and to be prepared

BELOW: *Ship Street Barracks, to the rear of the Castle, which provided some protection during the Rising*
LAWRENCE COLLECTION, NATIONAL LIBRARY OF IRELAND

for noise, as machine-guns were going to start. We groped round in pitch darkness, unable to see who was who, so it was hopeless to try and do anything – and then the guns began. Such a noise! It was well they had warned us. it was quite unlike any firing I had heard before, and varied from a rifle much as a cinema differs from a photograph. We comforted ourselves with the thought of the last of the Rebels' heels, and that in a few moments our seven hours' excitement would be over, and we should return to the status quo, but it was not long before we began to be undeceived.

The folding doors between the Supper Room and the Anteroom were shut across with some difficulty, so that our lights could be turned up again without being seen from the Yard. At the front of the hospital they were busy. Partly because of light and chiefly because of danger, the beds had to be moved from the Picture Gallery and Throne Room to St Patrick's Hall. the corridor of the Officer's Quarters, and the landing outside, which were at the back of the house.

The back door of the Supper Room Kitchen faces the Operating Theatre, and as both doors were open, I could see inside. In the middle of the floor a man was lying on mackintoshes in pools of blood; all round were wounded being stitched up or having haemorrhage stopped.

A VAD who had finished her work in the Still Room came upstairs and asked, 'What can I do to help? Couldn't I do anything in there?' and she pointed at the Theatre. I suggested they seemed already to have more nurses than patients; but she really wanted to be of use, to come in and talk to the men who were fearfully strung up: so we did.

The four empty beds in the ward were filled by men wounded that evening.

It must have been well after 10 p.m. when one of the men asked me if I had had anything to eat. I had quite forgotten till then that we had had no supper, but I was not hungry. Next time I went into the kitchen he produced a nice little pot of fresh tea, and lovely fingers of hot buttered toast, he had made for me. They looked really appetising, but I had only time to taste them: he sat over them like a watch-dog, and every time I appeared had them ready for me to take another bite.

About 11 p.m. the man with dislocation of the knee was carried in. When he was comfortably in bed, with hot jars and a good meal, I stayed to talk to him for a few minutes. I was interested to hear he was in the 4th Hussars, and inquired for several friends in that regiment who I heard were in the Yard. 'Did you know Mr P–?' he asked. 'He was killed out there, not long ago.' I almost felt as if I had been stunned – the dream had vanished – I was up against realities. That terrible noise, which even then I had only partly begun to connect in my mind with the wounded coming in, had meant the death of a man I knew. I suddenly realised how terribly tired I was, and was very glad of the tea and toast still waiting for me.

In the kitchen the nurses, and the men who had not gone to bed, were exchanging rumours and scraps of information they had gleaned. The machine-guns had not been entirely in our favour; we had only one to the Sinn Feiners' three. The City Hall had been stormed and taken; but the 'Evening Mail' office, opposite the Front Gate, was still in the hands of the Rebels. We also learnt that the trouble was spreading, and that the GPO, Jacob's, and other important buildings, were strongly held.

A jumble of thoughts passed through my mind, chiefly the adventures of the day. Civil war, so long expected and yet so unexpected, was actually an accomplished fact! One wondered how far it would spread, and how long it would last. I should have liked some news of my people, who live in Dublin; but 'bad news flies apace', and it is against my principles to worry about the unknown.

I was roused from my reverie by a violent shake. 'Get up and put on your coat; we must go into the hospital; it is too dangerous to stay here.' In spite of the truce till 4 a.m., sniping had been kept up continuously the whole night. I thought it was an official order, so reluctantly I dragged myself out of bed, put on a dressing-gown and my uniform coat. 'Do hurry! It is awfully dangerous; they are firing right at our windows.'

Our room was really a double one, with the partition knocked down, and had four windows, two looking out on the Yard, and two on the west side of the Castle. Opposite these side windows was a wall, at the top of a rise of ground, and it was from here the Sinn Feiners were firing down at the sentry, who was quite near our windows. I believe several sentries were killed there.

It was out of the question to cross the Yard. The only other way of getting into the hospital was by a back staircase, which was barricaded to prevent its being used.

The sniping still continued, but the shots were few and far between. A batch of wounded might arrive at any moment, as at 4.30 a.m. we had watched the troops march out of the Yard, with bayonets fixed, followed by the stretcher-bearers.

Except for a few visitors to our men in King Edward's House, it might have been an ordinary morning in the Supper Room – not so downstairs! The hall was turned into a receiving station, fitted up with screens;

supplies of bandages and dressings and kettles of boiling water were kept in readiness. The men's diningroom was packed, and the corridor thronged with soldiers waiting for breakfast. The crowd was so dense, it seemed hopeless to try to manoeuvre my tray through; but there were cries of 'Gangway! Gangway!' and a passage appeared as if by magic. Such a jolly, cheery crowd they were: one would almost have thought they liked coming up to Dublin to be shot at.

The men still had five meals in a day, but could only be spared one half slice of bread each at a meal. Sometimes it was dry; generally I was given a dish of jam or dripping each morning, and spread it on the bread myself to make it go as far as possible. There was always a good supply of meat at dinner. I think I am correct in saying it was brought in by a gentleman in his private car, at his own risk, his only protection being a red cross on his arm. Vegetables and puddings we forgot the look of; sugar ran out, and milk had to be treated as if it were as valuable as mercury, the supply was so irregular.

We had breakfasted three hours earlier than ordinary, so were looking forward to 10 o'clock lunch with more than usual zest. It was not a healthy, open-air hunger, but an unpleasant sensation of emptiness. At 10 a.m. came the news there was to be no lunch, so there was nothing for it but to imagine we had had it.

The Supper Room beds were all filled, so the newcomers were taken to other wards; but from the windows we could see a constant stream of ambulances and stretchers going in and out of the Yard – the dead had their faces covered.

During the afternoon the firing was intense. They said the Sinn Feiners were firing from a wall opposite, over our ward and kitchen, into the Castle Yard. I felt especially sorry for the new patients, who had friends in the thick of it.

In the kitchen the bullets seemed to be raining on the walls: time after time we looked round to see if the windows were broken, but we had a marvellous escape. There was a sniper just over us, and the whole room seemed to tremble each time he fired. A VAD on night duty made desperate efforts to sleep in one of the Sir Anthony Weldon wards, facing the same direction, but gave it up, as the bullets were hitting the wall in quick succession.

In the evening we watched the men in the Yard bombing the office of the 'Evening Mail'. The noise was terrific, but eventually the building was successfully stormed. From then on, we were considered comparatively safe.

That night the watch-fires were lit again in the Yard. So many of those who had stood around them the night before were now patients in our wards, or stretched stiff and cold. One wondered with a shudder how many more gaps another twenty-four hours would make.

A few more patients were brought to the Throne Room next day, two of them Sinn Feiners. One was an elderly man with grey hair, rather a commonplace individual; the other was a shrimp. Such a miserable little specimen, about five feet, without a pick of flesh on his bones! His teeth were literally chattering with fright, and he looked 'as if he had been up the chimney,' which was precisely where he had been! He was most anxious to keep up a flow of conversation, but that was too much of a luxury for Rebels (time was very precious); he was brought to us suffering from exhaustion. His pitiful appearance led me to ask why he had joined. 'It was all for show; we liked parading through the streets; we were told that was all we had to do, and I never thought of this – indeed, I never did, – and when we started on Monday morning, even then I thought it was all for show, till they suddenly ordered us to fire on any one in uniform, and then marched us off to take (I forgot which particular building he had come from), and I was so frightened I went up the chimney, and I had to stay there three days, and I never got a bit to eat, – oh! it was awful! and I never fired a shot – indeed, I never did.' That I quite believed, and as he stopped to take breath I made my escape. The Rebels must have been ordered to plead absolute ignorance, as it was always the same story. The only original answer we were given was: 'It would take too long to tell you now why I did it; but I'm going to do twelve years' penal servitude, and when I come out I'll tell you.'

The officers' dressing-room was turned into a 'dressing station,' where slight injuries were attended to: over two hundred and fifty cases were treated here. As the room was fitted with basins, several of us had to spend all spare moments there washing bandages and mackintoshes, which needless to say, were never ending. The

Matron had given out that any nurse who had the chance might sit down, so I used to pull a chair over to the basin and scrub away with my back turned to every one, oblivious to general conversation: it was very rude, but I was too tired to care.

The windows overlook the Castle garden, where all day about twenty men were digging graves. The nearest were for officers, each made separately; then two large graves for Tommies and civilians, and, far away by themselves, the Sinn Feiners. There were over seventy buried in the garden: most of them were removed when the

stiff, the hands so blue, and the faces covered. One wondered if they were the men had shouted 'Gangway!' that morning, and laughed and talked so cheerily.

It is also impossible to state chronologically the arrival of Sinn Fein prisoners. The only batch I clearly remember were fifteen or sixteen respectable-looking men, brought from the Four Courts the Tuesday morning after the Surrender. They were mostly elderly, and all but two wore red crosses on their arms. They showed more signs of curiosity than fear; but as we had heard that every man over eighteen was to be shot, we could not bear to look at them. They were marched round, and disappeared through a side door of Ship Street Barracks.

Captured ammunition was also brought into the Yard; one pile included a German officer's sword, a number of German rifles and dum-dum bullets.

The artillery rolled out from the Castle Yard to fulfil its deadly mission, and returned, sometimes within an hour, sometimes not till the evening. Fresh troops arrived from England; and, before they joined in the fighting, rested on the hard flags at the back, or the equally hard Yard in the

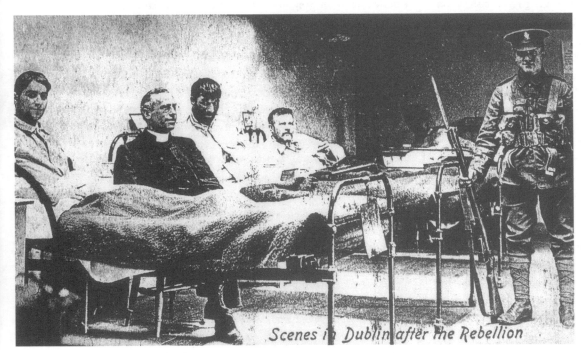

Scenes in Dublin after the Rebellion

Rebellion was over, but some of the officers are there still. Only a very limited number of coffins could be obtained: most of the bodies were buried sewn into sheets. The funerals took place each evening after dark: more than once the burying party was fired on. Towards the end of the week the dead were so many, they were brought in covered carts instead of ambulances. I saw a cart open once — about fifteen bodies, one on top of the other. It took time to carry them round to the Mortuary, 'and sometimes as one passed two or three bodies would be lying near the side door, dressed in khaki, but so still, so

front. Sometimes they looked so very tired.

Continual rumours reached us that the whole town was in flames, and that even the Rotunda had not escaped: we had a fleeting glimpse of the red flare in the sky as we ran across the Yard at night. There was also news that the Four Courts had been blown up, and that Jacob's Biscuit Factory was to share a like fate. Our own basement was carefully searched by officers, lest the Rebels should have thought of dynamiting us.

Frequently, when the men were resting in the Yard, there would be a stampede, and they would stand flattened against the walls – the Yard was under fire. Some men were wounded in it and several killed.

From the windows we could see a little of the fighting behind Ship Street. Soldiers on the roof of a large red building were bombing a house to the left; for some time after it was in a very shattered condition, and puffs of smoke issuing through the gaps in the roof showed that Sinn Feiners had not yet deserted it.

Teas were being brought, and high good-humour prevailed over the toast, when some one hurled herself in with: 'The Rebels have surrendered unconditionally!' We could hardly believe our ears; it seemed much too wonderful to be true.

The news was followed by a damper: 'Thirty new nurses have arrived – what are they to eat? I should rather do twice as much again than have rations cut down any further.' We echoed the sentiment. It did not occur to us, that once surrender was official, we should be able to get plenty of food.

A new nurse and two VADs were sent to the Throne Room; other wards received similar reinforcements, and we had the unexpected experience of tumbling over each other. The arrival of James Connolly caused an unusual stir. From the window I could see him lying on the stretcher, his hands crossed, his head hidden from us by the archway. The stretcher was on the ground, and at either side stood three of his officers, in National Volunteer Uniform; a guard of about thirty soldiers stood around. The scene did not change for ten minutes or more; somebody gruesomely suggested they were discussing whether he should be brought in, or if it would be better to shoot him at once. It is more likely they were arranging where he should be brought, and a small ward in the Officers' Quarters, where he could be carefully guarded, was decided upon.*

The nurses in charge of him acknowledged, without exception, that he was entirely different from their expectations: no one could have been more considerate, or have given less trouble. About a week after his arrival he had an operation on the leg. He was strongly opposed to this himself, but until he had been tried, he had to be treated entirely from a medical point of view. When he was coming round after the ether, the sentry changed, and

he turned to the nurse who was minding him and asked, 'Have they come to take me away? Must I really die so soon?' All through, his behaviour was that of an idealist. He was calm and composed during the court-martial, and said, 'You can shoot me if you like, but I am dying for my country.' He showed no sign of weakness till his wife was brought to say good-bye to him, the night he was to be shot. When she had left, he saw the monks, and about 3 a.m. he was carried down on a stretcher to the ambulance that was to bring him to Kilmainham.

At 6.30 p.m., the charm of an idle life and the prospect of a reasonable amount of sleep had not lost their first gloss, when my staff nurse mentioned a rumour that I was to go on to night duty. At first I thought she was joking, but as she really meant it, I had to find out if it were true. After some time I met the Assistant Matron with a list in her hand: 'You are being changed, and are to go on to night duty I think – yes – here it is – night duty in the Picture Gallery. So run off as quickly as you can, and lie down for an hour; you must be on duty again at 8 o'clock.'

Upstairs, bustle and business ruled in the Picture Gallery. Since the firing had stopped, the ambulances could drive through the streets in safety, and a great number of wounded were brought in.

About 9 p.m. the day staff retired, and left one staff nurse, one probationer, and me to look after the twenty-seven patients.

I never thought I should have seen such suffering as was in that ward that night; the groaning was indescribable. One man was shot through the head; they said his brains were showing, and that if he lived he would be insane. He made a marvellous recovery. There was a man who had just had an arm amputated; another had his arm terribly smashed up with a poisoned wound the size of a tennis-ball – for several days they feared they would have to amputate; another had an equally damaged leg. One had a dressing over the whole side of his face, with thick clots of blood at the edges; I heard that half his face was gone, and never passed him without a prayer he

*Prior to the Rising Connolly had turned down a proposal to burn Dublin Castle because this Red Cross hospital was within its precincts.

might not live. Providence was wiser than I; his face, though frightfully disfigured, was not blown away, and within a week he became one of the cheeriest men in the ward, and one of the most particular as to the set of his hair! All that night he made no sign of consciousness, except when, with his uninjured eye still closed, he fumbled for his drinking-cup, which he could only manage by a tube put into his mouth. Then there was a boy in the South Staffords, with the blue face one dreaded to see. Normally he must have been unusually good-looking, and he was not more than eighteen. Every few minutes he would sit bolt upright, stripped to the waist, and stare wildly round with unseeing eyes; and when we tried to make him lie down again, would shrink from being touched, and grunt his disapproval. I came into the ward just in time to see screens being put round a bed – it was the first time I had ever seen the face of a dead man.

The Sinn Feiners in the ward made me feel worst of all; we still believed all Rebels over eighteen were to be shot. I had felt very stony to the ones in the Throne Room, but these were different, – they were so ill, so weak, so helpless. I could have cried, it seemed so cruel to drag them through such torture … the time passed quickly, as the men were very restless; many of them needed their dressings changed, and all wanted their pillows turned and a drink at least every five minutes; most of them needed injections of morphia. About midnight some of them showed signs of quieting down. The staff nurse discovered I had been on duty since 6 a.m., so she made me sit in a big chair by the fire, and promised to tell me if she wanted me. When I stood up again, I felt as if I had acute rheumatism all over, and could hardly walk; it was so painful, I did not give my muscles another chance to stiffen. We had dinner, about eight of us together, at the table outside the Officers' Quarters. A memorable spread: poached eggs and bacon, plenty of bread, and our greedy eyes fixed on a dish of butter.

When I awoke about 6.30 p.m. it was hard to believe it was Sunday, and only a week since Easter Day.

We were at dinner in the kitchen, when a stretcher-bearer offered us his newspaper, the now famous paper with three dates. It was the first communication we had held with the outside world for over a week, and we nearly tore it to pieces in our excitement. Such, however, is the frailty of human nature, it was not other peoples' experiences which thrilled us most, but to see how vivid a picture of our adventures had been drawn for the world in general. We expected something similar to accounts of the Siege of Derry, but we had some difficulty in finding it. 'There was a faint-hearted attack on Dublin Castle, which resulted in the shooting of one policeman.' That was all! We still hoped for some recognition of the nursing world, and were not disappointed: 'The civilians behaved with wonderful calmness, as also did the doctors and nurses.' It was all right to put the doctors above us, – but the civilians – who, we thought, had either run like rabbits to their holes, or risked their skins for nothing but curiosity! What a mercy Providence has not shut us off permanently from the outer world, or what limits would our egotism not reach!

From *Blackwood's Magazine* (December 1916).

CHAPTER THIRTEEN

THE CASTLE AND THE NEW NATION

The last Lord Lieutenant of Ireland was Viscount FitzAlan, the first Catholic Viceroy permitted by law since Tyrconnell died in 1691. He was one of the Duke of Norfolk's family, the leading Catholic family in England, and though he had been Tory chief whip it was thought that as a Catholic he would be welcome. But as was remarked at the time, the Irish 'would as soon welcome a new Catholic hangman as a Catholic Viceroy they didn't want'.

During FitzAlan's time in Ireland, threats against his life meant he could not even go out to Mass. His coat of arms had been added to the series of arms of the Viceroys in the Chapel Royal, but it was observed that they filled the very last space available, on the side of Communion Table, a truly symbolic fact.

On 16 January 1922, FitzAlan welcomed Michael Collins, a young man in a hurry, who arrived at Dublin Castle in a taxi. Collins and his colleagues produced the signed copy of the Treaty, which the Viceroy accepted. The Provisional Government of the Irish Free State was now duly recognised.

A brief communiqué was later issued: 'The members of Rialtas Sealadach na h-Éireann (the Provisional Government of Ireland) received the

ABOVE: *The last Viceroy, Lord FitzAlan, arriving to hand over the Castle in January 1922*

surrender of Dublin Castle at 1.45 p.m. yesterday. It is now in the hands of the Irish Nation.'

Republican opponents of the new government noted, however, that the whole of this historic ceremony, concluding seven centuries of British rule, had been conducted away from the eyes of the press. The Provisional Government issued a proclamation on its own authority instructing the courts and civil service to continue to function as before, but under new auspices.

General Boyd, the commander of the remaining British forces in the Free State, now moved his headquarters from Dublin Castle to Phoenix Park, and all

RIGHT: *Michael Collins arrives by taxi, as ever in a hurry, to accept the surrender of the great symbol of British rule to the new state*

BELOW: *The last social event of the old order: a children's Christmas party*
IRISH LIFE

over the country British troops were now being slowly withdrawn, and replaced by the National Army of Collins and Griffith. But in some areas the new soldiers were Republicans.

On 17 August 1922, again as part of the Treaty arrangements, the police quarters at Dublin Castle were

handed over to men of the new Civic Guard. The new Commissioner of the Guards, Michael Staines, claimed a month later: 'The Civic Guard will succeed not by force of arms, or numbers, but on their moral authority as servants of the people.'

Lord FitzAlan departed. One of his last acts was

to send a message to the newly-assembled Dáil on 9 September 1922, saying that the Parliament had his best wishes and prayers. On 5 December, the King appointed Tim Healy, the old enemy of Parnell, as Governor-General. And so the Viceroys passed into history.

The last social event at Dublin Castle was a children's Christmas party in 1922, held for youngsters who would be among the first citizens of the new Ireland.

* * *

The RIC, which had been based at Dublin Castle, was disbanded in January 1923, and recruiting for the new Civic Guards went on apace. The Castle and the Ship Street barracks behind it were the new depot, and most of the new recruits were moved there. The new men fell to their duties without much training, guarding the Castle, government buildings and the city centre banks. Once the Republicans threw a bomb over the wall into the barracks, though they later apologised for this. The recruits were later removed to Phoenix Park, but the Commissioner's Office remained at the Castle – except for the detectives. The Criminal Investigation Department was now to be located at Oriel House (33–34 Westland Row), from where surveillance and pursuit of Republicans would be undertaken during the

Civil War and its aftermath. This group was not formally a part of the new police at all, and though they had been effective in the war against the political subversives, they were not, it was thought, well suited to more peaceful times.

In October 1923 they were disbanded, and thirty-one of them (all ex-IRA men) were transferred to the G Division of the DMP. The Dublin police remained at the Castle, though in 1925 the DMP ceased to exist and a unified Civic Guard (rather than a gendarmerie) came into existence. In 1925 they were further divided into the Detective branch and the Special Branch. These were armed, and now included not only the men from Oriel House but also army officers. Under central control from Dublin Castle they dealt with political crime throughout the country during the remaining years of the Cosgrave government, which was replaced (peacefully) by de Valera's in 1932.

In 1932, to face the threat of the Blueshirt movement and in particular its 'March On Dublin' in August 1932, sixty men were recruited from Fianna Fáil party ranks to swell the Special Branch at Dublin Castle. In the event the march was called off. More men were recruited, however, and – known as 'Broy's Harriers' (from the Garda commissioner Col. Eamon Broy) – they prevented the sort of street politics that was sweeping Europe with the rise of Fascism. Once Dublin Castle had seemed the bastion of British repression. Now many Republicans, Radicals and Communists felt not much had changed. The Special Branch shared the Castle with the Post Office telephone engineers, and suspicions of telephone tapping were rife in some city circles from the 1940s onwards. Two tappers were caught at work by Séan MacBride on 19 February 1948, his first day as a government minister.

* * *

Dublin Castle was taken over by the Free State government, which soon found itself embroiled in the events of the Civil War. The Executive decided, however, that it would not settle there. Leinster House (which belonged to the RDS) was taken over for an Assembly, and the government departments were more conveniently relocated in adjacent buildings in Upper Merrion Street, where they have remained ever since. The new nation seemed to be turning its back on Dublin Castle.

But after the destruction of the Four Courts in

LEFT: *British troops in Dublin Castle cheering their officers on their departure from Ireland*

the summer of 1922 the High Court was removed on a temporary basis to the Castle. (It would be eight years until the Four Courts re-opened on 5 October 1931.) The Duke of Dorset, remarked Thomas Ulick Sadleir at this time, when he placed the statues of Justice and Fortitude over the gates of the Castle in 1753, little dreamed that in 1923 the only gateway still in use would be that surmounted by the smiling figure of Justice, 'now so fittingly looking down upon her Courts. And when Justice comes at last into her own, surely a happy era is at hand'.

Among the routine business of the High Court during these years was one case which focused the attention of the wider world on the Castle. This was the civil action described on the docket as 'In the matter of the goods of Richard Croker deceased'. 'Boss' Croker was the notorious Irish-American politician, whose rule of iron over local New York politics from Tammany Hall had become a byword for corruption. He had retired first to Britain and then to Ireland, where he was made a Freeman of Dublin in July 1907 – whatever Yankee Wasps may have thought of him, at home in Ireland he was a hero. He gained further fame as a horse breeder, the owner of Orby the famous Derby winner. He was married a second time to a Cherokee Indian princess, and when he died his children by his first wife sued for a share of his estates in Ireland and the United States.

The case opened on 20 April 1923 in the High Court over probate of the will. The court was crowded to capacity every day. The hearings began on 31 May and continued for two weeks with sensational evidence alleging that the second Mrs Croker was not what she claimed to be, and had actually been married to an Italian plumber. The case ended on 15 June, with the Irish jury finding in Mrs Croker's favour. A large and excited crowd of Dubliners cheered to the echo as she left Dublin Castle in triumph. After further legal work, on 24 August probate of the will of Richard Croker was granted to his executor Bula E. Croker: he left in Ireland an estate of a mere £150, his personal jewellery and apparel at Glencairn, his country house.

The Law Library, where the barristers met their clients' solicitors, was in St Patrick's Hall, while the supreme courts sat in the Throne Room, the Council Chamber and the State Apartments, with No. 5 Court in the Bermingham Tower. The Courts continued to sit in Dublin Castle until October 1931 when, after an interval of eight years, the judges and lawyers returned to their ancient haunts across the river. This judicial use of the Castle, which had begun in the Middle Ages, was a prime purpose of the place which has been revived in more recent years.

* * *

With the end of the Civil War Ireland became generally more settled, though the police found that they had a more turbulent city to deal with from Dublin Castle in the post-war years. It was not only crime, encouraged by the ex-servicemen and ex-irregulars, but also new influences from abroad. Of course by comparison with America or Europe the incidents were of no great significance.

On 1 February 1928, James MacNeill (the brother of Eoin MacNeill, who had been Irish High Commissioner in London) was sworn in as Governor-General in succession to Tim Healy at a ceremony in Dublin Castle. But for most of the time the Castle slumbered, awakening only occasionally for special events. One such was a state reception on 21 June 1932 for the Papal legate to the 31st Eucharistic Congress, His Eminence Cardinal Lorenzo Lauri. To many of the older generation the Congress was one of the special events of memory, and one into which the new state poured its meagre resources. Yet oddly, in the perspective of time, this was the watershed, for it could be argued that it was from this date that the influence of the Catholic Church in public life began slowly to decline (despite the new constitution in 1937).

Though the Cosgrave government had attempted to add some colour to the public life of the state, high ceremony was not much favoured by the new régime of Mr de Valera which had come to power shortly before. When Donal Buckley, or Domhnall Ua Buachalla as he preferred to call himself, was sworn in before the Chief Justice on 26 November 1932, it was admitted by the government that he would not have much of a role in the nation's public life. Pride of place would be reserved for Mr de Valera, of course. Buckley did not even move into the Park.

However, when distinguished guests arrived from abroad no effort was spared. When the Australian Premier J.A. Lyons came to Ireland in 1935, he was entertained at a lavish affair in Dublin Castle on 11 May.

Things were changing. The IRA was banned as an illegal organisation on 19 June 1936, a mere month after the final meeting of the old Senate of the Free State. This had been abolished under the new Constitution which came into force in 1937. Though the Gaelicisation of Ireland was close to de Valera's heart, he was also able to dedicate the new Reading Room at Trinity College, showing in a small way that Protestants also had a part in the new state.

On 25 June 1938 Dr Douglas Hyde, the Anglo-Irish founder of the Gaelic League and son of a rector, was inaugurated in St Patrick's Hall as the first President of Ireland. That evening the Prime Minister and Mrs de Valera hosted a state reception in Dublin in honour of this historic event.

A feature of many of the state events was the Blue Hussars, the mounted escort of the President, set up in 1931. These descended, of course, from the cavalry unit of the old Viceroy, which had been stationed in the Park (and which is featured in *Ulysses*, escorting Lord Dudley on his progress through the city). The Irish Army was intensely proud of its horsemen, so that even when the troop, in all its Ruritanian quaintness, was abolished by the government in 1948 'to save money', the equestrian corps continues to compete internationally. But the going of the Hussars removed a dash of old-fashioned colour, and soldiers on motor cycles were no substitute.

ABOVE: *The famous Blue Hussars, the official Irish horse guards of the 1920s*

* * *

In the early 1930s Elizabeth, Countess of Fingall, then living in a small flat off Mespil Road, was beginning the task of dictating her memoirs to Pamela Hinkson. Her mind went back through the decades to her own first Season at Dublin Castle, and she called into the Genealogical Office there to try to restore her memories, and recover the feelings of the old days.

The other day I went to the Castle, and in the Herald's Office, that last survivor of a world which kept and treasured tradition and such things, we took down the Dinner Book and the Drawing Room Book of that time. The immense leather-covered records had remained undisturbed for years and had to have the dust wiped from them.

Dust over those names!

I found Lord and Lady Ormonde there, from Kilkenny Castle, and Lady Brook, and the Duchess of Leinster of that day, the Ladies Fitzgerald, from Carton. And the Marquis and Marchioness of Kildare, from Kilkea Castle — and many other names that I remembered. There was, surprisingly, Mr. George Moore, Moore Hall, Co. Mayo, staying at the Shelbourne Hotel, a young man up from the bogs and lakes of Mayo for the Dublin Season. And I find Madame MacDermott and myself,

Miss Burke, Buswell's Hotel.

We put the records back for the dust to cover them again.

from *Seventy Years Young. Memories of Elizabeth, Countess of Fingal* (1936)

* * *

With the coming of the Free State the Castle's significance declined. In 1922 the Lower Yard, for instance, housed the Offices of the Ordnance Department, the Quartermaster General, the Treasury Buildings, the residence of the Master of the Horse, Riding Schools and the Stables. By 1928 the departments housed in Dublin Castle included the General Prisons Board, Reformatory and Industrial schools, Paymaster General's Office, Inland Revenue Office, Commissioner of Police Office, Castle Police Barracks, General Post Office secretary's office, Department of Industry and Commerce, and the General Post Office Engineers and savings bank.

A mid-century directory records the following offices there. In the Lower Castle Yard: Military Church of the Holy Trinity, Department of Industries and Commerce, Statistics, Claims and Record Office, Gas Weights and Measures, Office Keeper's quarters, Office of Works (Stores etc.), Civic Guard Offices, Civic Guard Barracks, Assay Office, Office of the Revenue Commissioners including Accountant General of Revenue, Estate Duty Office, Registry of Business Names, and Offices of Chief Inspector of Customs and Excise, Chief Inspector of Taxes and Registration Office. In the Upper Castle Yard were the Guard House, Genealogical Office, Revenue Commissioners, and Office of Special Commissioners of Income Tax, Stamp Office and Chief State Solicitors Office. Off Ship Street was the Telephone Department of the General Post Office.

Whatever may have been its central role under the old administration, in the new Ireland Dublin Castle remained as busy as ever. It was also a useful place for finding offices for any novel scheme at short notice. It was in the Castle that the Minister of Justice Gerald Boland set up the new Children's Courts after he took office in September 1939. He had always opposed the notion of young offenders (or juvenile delinquents as they were called in those days) being tried in the criminal courts. In the new Children's Court the sitting were held in an entirely different atmosphere: the justices did not wear their robes, the police were not in uniform, and their location in Dublin Castle was far removed from the ordinary courts on the other side of the Liffey.

During the first years of World War II, Dublin Castle played a significant role in the defence of the country. The situation in the city was very tense. The traditional Easter ceremonies by Republicans were banned. Over a thousand were to be interned, nine executed, six killed in shoot-outs, and three to die on hunger strike. In April 1940 two of these hunger strikers, held in Mountjoy Gaol, died. In retaliation the IRA attacked Dublin Castle. A former Republican member of Broy's Harriers, now disillusioned with the Special Branch and its activities, helped IRA GHQ make contact with a clerk inside the Castle. The plan was to destroy the radio store in the Castle in the Lower Castle Yard, so hampering Special Branch communications. Crofton, the ex-policeman, opened up a way in for the IRA using huge wire-clippers he had hidden down his back. But the bomb squad, when they arrived later, placed the bomb in the wrong room. It seriously wounded five of the Special Branch and the Castle Housekeeper.

This was the last actual act of war against Dublin Castle, but it was also an act of war against the Irish state, and an act unlikely to gain much favour with the general public, though it emphasised that for Republicans the Castle still remained a symbol of the enemy. But de Valera, with the support of W.T. Cosgrave the leader of the Opposition, remained resolute in the face of such threats. The IRA were worsted in the struggle with the state, but Dublin Castle (as we shall see) was to benefit by de Valera's interest.

Also in 1940, with the outbreak of actual war, the basement of the old Under Secretary's Office, by the gate into the Upper Yard, was taken over as a keypoint in the anti-aircraft defences of the capital. This was, of course, before radar or supersonic planes. A great plotting table was set up, on which the flight paths of planes reported by anti-aircraft gun posts around Dublin could be traced. Above it, in a sort of glass-fronted bridge, the commanders could follow what was going on, sending out orders to the AA positions to open fire if it looked as if a full-scale attack was under way.

Dogfights between German and British fighters were seen from time to time over the city, but less entertaining events also occurred. On 2–3 January 1941 German bombs fell on Rathdown Park in Terenure and Donore Terrace, Dolphin's Barn, and though there was much damage to property, no one was killed. Later that year, on 31 May, four high-explosive bombs were dropped on the North Strand area, killing some thirty-seven people and injuring eighty. Whether this was deliberate, or whether the pilots thought they were over Belfast, was uncertain, but after the war Germany – which had been supporting the IRA in their efforts to subvert the Irish state – paid Ireland £327,000 in compensation.

There was a sad footnote to the war years a little later, one of the most dramatic incidents in recent times at the Castle. Herman Goertz had been Germany's main agent and contact with the IRA during the early years of the war. He had been arrested by the Special Branch and interned. After the war he was released and went into business, but he lived in fear of being deported back to Germany, where he felt he would face imprisonment, or even execution. He was obliged to report periodically to the Aliens' Registration Office in the Castle, and on the morning of 23 May 1947 he presented himself as usual. But this time he was told he would be detained later that day, with the implication that he would be repatriated.

Goertz thanked the detective sergeant who gave him this news, but he remained sitting quietly in the waiting room, smoking his pipe. He was due to see his solicitor at 10.30 a.m. One of the two policemen in the room realised at 10.15 that Goertz was taking something. He tried to stop him, wrenching from his hand a small glass phial. He asked him what it was, and Goertz said it was none of his business. Nothing happened for a few seconds and then the former spy collapsed. The two policemen called an ambulance to the Castle, and did what they could for him in the

meantime. Goertz was pronounced dead at Mercer's Hospital an hour later. He was found to have taken a dose of potassium cyanide – the secret agent's death.

Soon after, at the commission of inquiry, one of the members, John A. Costello, later leader of the first Inter-party government in 1948, pleaded that they should say nothing in reporting on the suicide at Dublin Castle that reflected on Goertz's sense of honour as a German soldier. This sensational episode in the Castle's history ended with a funeral in Deansgrange cemetery attended by members of the IRA.

Early in 1941, Ireland was faced with the serious possibility of invasion either by Germany, or by the Allies (already established in the north). Only adroit diplomacy averted this. By 1942 the whole air-raid set-up was moved elsewhere. Dublin Castle might well have slumbered again. But, perhaps as a result of the IRA attack, a greater interest in the Castle, the State Apartments, the Chapel Royal and the Genealogical Office was shown by the Government, which was effectively Eamon de Valera.

In 1943, the oldest Office of State in Ireland, the office of Ulster King-of-Arms founded in 1552, ceased to be an office of the British State, and was transferred by the Irish government to the National Library (then under Dr Richard Hayes) where it became the Genealogical Office. It remained, however, in the Bedford Tower in Dublin Castle. The Deputy Ulster at this time was the scholar Thomas Ulick Sadleir. De Valera visited the new offices and was duly photographed poring over the ancient parchments of achievement.

In the Middle Ages the heralds' duties formerly comprised the regulation of armorial bearings, the ordering of tournaments, trials by combat, the arrangement of state ceremonies, and the bearers of royal messages. In Ireland they established such things as the order of precedence at official functions under the Viceroy. Their main duty in modern times, however, consists of devising and granting coats-of-arms, and the authentication of pedigrees. Indeed, one of their first acts under the aegis of the Free State was to provide a coat of arms for Dublin County Council! In Ireland, as the change of name implied, they became a major source of historical information not only about the titled nobility, but also the landed gentry and the hereditary chiefs of Gaelic Ireland.

Since 1922 no new knights had been appointed except the Extra Royal Knights, the Duke of Windsor in 1927 and the Duke of Gloucester in 1934. There were nineteen vacancies. The last non-royal appointment had been the Duke of Abercorn in 1922. Republicans

Roman Catholic bishops, remains important, a herald in an embroidered tabard and gold chains was no longer required.

The Chief Herald, Dr Edward MacLysaght, was a distinguished writer and scholar, as was his assistant and successor Gerard Slevin. The Heraldic Museum then had as Trustees Terence Gray, Thomas Ulick Sadleir. and Major Guillamore O'Grady.

Far from being a mere feudal relic, the

RIGHT: *Fire Brigade officers inspect the aftermath of the fire in Dublin Castle in 1941*
IRISH INDEPENDENT

regarded all this machinery as so much feudal mumbo-jumbo. However, those involved in the Office of Arms were deeply scholarly men and have continued to be so. But, though the provision of coats of arms, mainly to

Genealogical Office became a tourist attraction and of increasing importance as the years went by. The loss in the Civil War of the Records Office (mined by the Republicans) has placed an even greater value on such papers as survived elsewhere, as in the Office of Arms. Bound up in these records is the whole history of Ireland running right back to the origins of the Gaelic chieftains, some fifteen of whom are officially recognised by the Irish State, the genuine aristocrats of the Irish Republic. To any person at all sensitive to the nuances of Irish history, and Mr de Valera was more sensitive than most, this place was the one national treasure in Dublin Castle.

* * *

Whether in peace or war, all of these offices in Dublin Castle represented quite an array of civil servants and officials!

Indeed it was largely to cater for these people that the Chapel Royal, disused since 1922, was re-dedicated as the military Church of the Holy Trinity (for Catholic services) by the Primate of Ireland, de Valera's close friend the Archbishop of Dublin, Dr John Charles McQuaid, on 4 June 1944. Mass had not been said in the Castle (so it was said in a guidebook published a little earlier in the year by Harold Leask of the OPW) since James II passed through Dublin in flight from William of Orange after the Battle of the Boyne! Viscount FitzAlan had attended Mass either in the pro-Cathedral, or in his own chapel in the Viceregal Lodge. The re-dedication was therefore received with great satisfaction by many national-minded people.

The original gothic-style organ in the Chapel

Royal was removed to the Church of Ireland church in Waterford, where it remains. The ceiling was painted a dark, night-sky blue with gold stars, a very Catholic scheme in contrast to what had been intended (in the usual Church of Ireland style) to have been a severely plain treatment. A set of Stations of the Cross, carved by the monks of Glenstal Abbey from native Irish woods, were hung on the wall, where they still remain, a slightly incongruous Roman item in the newly-restored Anglican chapel.

In January 1941 there had been a serious fire in State Apartments. The damage was extensive enough, but it also provided an opportunity for Raymond McGrath, the multi-talented chief architect of the Board of Works, to undertake renovations and restorations. He had in fact plans for a far more radical scheme for both the Upper and Lower Castle Yards but, as was so often the case, these were not carried through.

RIGHT: Princess Grace of Monaco on her visit to Dublin Castle

This scheme was to have involved a curved building running across and around the lower yard connecting the entrance with the Castle garden. It was to have had four storeys and radiating blocks to the rear, all with a view over the south of the city. From their offices on the upper floors the senior civil servants would be able to overlook the Castle lawn, which was to fill the Lower Yard. There were to be new steps leading up to the cross block arch. A great deal of work went into the plans for this scheme at the OPW, but it was the object of a great deal of public criticism in 1947–8, a period when money was of more concern than appearance. It was nevertheless approved by the Inter-Party Government of J.A. Costello, but died away when de Valera came back to power in the 1950s.

Some of McGrath's work did survive, however. The State Apartments were in two parts, one fronting onto the Castle garden to the rear (the creation of Sir William Robinson in 1685), the other onto the Upper Yard. Investigations had shown that the cross block had been built in the eighteenth century over the moat, and that the uneven subsidence was literally breaking the back of the building.

Restoration of the damage began with the rebuilding during 1961–4 of the cross block, where interesting archaeological finds were made. The Presence Chamber which had stood alongside the Throne Room, was done away with. But the Drawing Room was restored completely as it had been, and was fitted with the pier glasses and console tables that had been rescued from the fire in 1941. An opportunity was taken to instal in the Apollo Room a ceiling from a demolished Georgian mansion off St Stephen's Green. When McGrath was finished, the State Apartments had taken on the appearance which they have retained to this day, though more building work was undertaken in recent years. Raymond McGrath also designed the new carpets, made for the Castle in Donegal, which successfully re-interpreted the classical modes of the building into a modern artifact. In due course a silver medal from the Royal Institute of Architects in Ireland was awarded to Oscar Richardson, J.B. Maguire and Raymond McGrath for the restoration of the Castle. Their work effectively brought its ancient fabric into modern times.

CHAPTER FOURTEEN

THE CASTLE IN MODERN TIMES

The death of Dr Douglas Hyde, the first President of Ireland, in 1945 gave rise to an embarrassing situation when those officers of state who were Catholics felt that they could not attend the Church of Ireland burial service in St Patrick's Cathedral. Such a thing now seems unthinkable. That it was ever possible seems even stranger.

On 25 June 1945 Seán T. O'Kelly (after a three-way race with Seán MacEoin of Fine Gael and the Republican Dr Patrick McCartan) was sworn in as the second President of Ireland. He remained in office until 1959, but was very much a lay figure, spending much of his time at his country home in Wicklow. During his terms of office, J.A. Costello decided it was time that Ireland became a republic in name as well as in reality.

On 18 April 1949, the Republic of Ireland was proclaimed in Dublin. This effectively removed any last vestige of the British order in Irish public life. Yet the

BELOW: *The inauguration of President de Valera in 1959*

old banners remained in place in Dublin Castle, and even now when the presidents attend services in St Patrick's Cathedral, and take communion there (as is often the case in these ecumenical days), they are placed in the old Viceroy's Stall beneath the Royal Standard. But this itself merely reflects the complex texture of Irish life and history.

From time to time the Castle still saw unusual ceremonies. One of these, on 11 May 1959, was the presentation to the Castle Chapel by the French government of copies of the banners of the Irish regiments that had fought in the Battle of Fontenoy (30 April 1745

churches in Ireland held British banners, here were some triumphant Irish battle honours for a change.

In the summer of 1959 Eamon de Valera was sworn in as the third President at Dublin Castle. His retirement from active politics seems to many to have marked the end of an era. Ireland had at last emerged from her revolutionary years. This was emphasised by the new direction initiated by Seán Lemass. The following decades would see a great many changes.

One change was in attitudes towards what constituted Irish heritage. No longer would it be considered merely the Celtic and Gaelic past. Georgian and Victorian Ireland now came to be appreciated in their own right, as increasing scholarship marched hand in hand with changing tastes and increasing wealth. Battle banners and royal standards were even less likely to be removed, as these were marks of a history that no amount of tinkering with today could alter.

Dublin Castle played a part in this change. Here the Republic could entertain its royal visitors. Though there had been many royal visits in the previous century, royalty was a rare thing in twentieth-century Ireland, although the Catholic rulers of the Belgians were entertained at the Castle when de Valera was President. So too were Prince Rainier of

ABOVE: *The visit of the King and Queen of the Belgians, with Mr and Mrs Jack Lynch*

Old Style, 11 May New Style) at which the ailing Marshal Saxe eventually defeated the English and their allies with the loss of 12,000 men in what one historian called 'an obstinate sanguinary battle'. Though many

Monaco and his new wife Princess Grace (formerly Miss Grace Kelly of Philadelphia). These visits were a new phenomenon in the Republic, an indication of Ireland opening out onto the wider world.

This made all the more reason to have the Castle presentable. During the 1961–2 season, excavations under the cross block were conducted under the direction of M. Ó hEochaidh of the Office of Public

Works, during which the older buildings were demolished as a prelude to rebuilding the cross block. The dig revealed deeply stratified layers of occupation going back through the Middle Ages to Viking times. The earliest level was from the tenth century. Parts of the medieval eastern and northern curtain walls and the north-eastern corner tower (the Powder Tower) were uncovered and recorded, though this dig is still unreported. Pottery shards from the thirteenth century as well as animal bones, oyster shells and other refuse were found, along with the waterlogged fragments of planked pavements and wicker screens, as well as pre-Norman barlip pottery and a tenth-century strap tag. These were exciting discoveries as it had been thought that there was very little to be found under Dublin due to the extensive rebuilding over the centuries.

LEFT: *Signing the roll after being made a Freeman of the City of Dublin*

BELOW: *President John F. Kennedy at Dublin Castle ceremonies during his state visit in 1963*

The Castle wall was some seventeen feet (five metres) thick, and a previously unknown secret staircase was found running through it, the steps of which can now be seen. The excavations were followed by the complete rebuilding of the eastern cross block, followed by a large segment of the east wing of the State Apartments in 1964–8. Thus the room which is today shown to visitors as that in which James Connolly, the Socialist leader of the Easter Rising, was detained, actually dates from this period. Though the interior may be deceptive in its restored appearance, the external brickwork clearly reveals to the eye its modern origin.

FAR RIGHT: *Visitors to the Castle now come in increasing numbers*

A part of Ireland's new image of itself was the visit of President Kennedy in 1963, a stirring historical occasion, for Kennedy was the epitome of the 'returned

RIGHT: *The arch leading to the Castle Steps*

Yank' of rural folklore. At a ceremony in St Patrick's Hall on 28 June, he was awarded honorary degrees by the Irish universities (Ireland's only acceptable form of public honours), and was granted the Freedom of the City of Dublin. He was followed in due course by General de Gaulle, in June 1969. Other distingushed visitors included the Rainiers of Monaco and the Belgian Royal family.

De Valera retired as President in June 1973, and died in August 1979 at the age of 92. It marked the end of an era. The 1970s saw a succession of presidents with Childers (1973, died in office 1974), Ó Dálaigh (1974, resigned 1976), and Hillery (1976). With inaugurations of all these following rapidly upon each other in the course of four years, Dublin Castle had not seen such ceremony since the old viceregal days when de Valera had been a mere boy.

CHAPTER FIFTEEN

THE RESURGENT CASTLE

By now the search was on for Dublin's buried past, with which the history of the Castle was inextricably linked.

Between 1962 and 1975, A.B. Ó Ríordáin conducted excavations at High Street, Winetavern Street, Christchurch Place and Fishamble Street. On these sites in the heart of the old city his team made some remarkable discoveries. But these excavations were overshadowed by the extraordinary finds by Patrick Wallace and his colleagues at Woodquay, Fishamble Street and John's Lane. These investigations brought to light the full vista of the Viking city between AD 900 and 1100.

These digs, however, were limited in area. Nothing has as yet been done around the site where the ford over the Liffey may have been, in the immediate area of Dublin Castle, or below it, in the area of the sanctuary around St Michael de la Pole. There is a great deal more still to be learned about pre-Viking Dublin.

In the meantime, all was not well in the Castle itself. The increasing public interest in heritage matters meant that it, too, came under closer scrutiny. A new office block, which to most eyes was very intrusive, was built on the site of the old stables; it was long occupied by the equally intrusive Revenue Commissioners. St George's Hall was renovated and adapted as a conference centre for Ireland's first presidency of the European Union in 1975. In 1980 the Chapel Royal had to be closed to the public due to structural decay. This did not pass without comment in the press, nor did the general condition of the other buildings in the Castle confines.

The Wood Quay Saga, between 1973 and 1983, in which massive efforts were made permanently to preserve the excavated remains, brought Viking Dublin properly alive for most people. Though this recent emphasis on 'Viking Dublin' cast the earlier Celtic settlement and the later Norman city into the shade, it also led to further work at Dublin Castle.

In the autumn of 1986 archaeological excavations began at the Castle and continued into the following year. As the new developments planned by the Office of Public Works were to be sited over the medieval moat, Ann Lynch and Conleth Manning, who undertook the initial archaeological investigation, were able to excavate only three small areas of pre-Norman strata. These were a small area outside the curving corner of the moat in the north-west corner of the Castle, a narrow strip inside the north curtain wall back to the cross block, and the circular area around the foundations of the Powder Tower.

At the first site, up to one metre of pre-Norman 'organic deposits' were excavated, bringing to light small houses of the same type as those already found at Wood Quay. In the second area there were two metres of deposits, but here the organic remains were poorly preserved although they found areas of cobbling and lines of port-holes.

In the third area a series of earthen defences predating the Castle were found. These were the eastern defences of the pre-Norman town along the bank of the Poddle estuary. The earliest of these was a mud bank with a sloping stone facing against which the river waters would have lapped. This was preserved, and can be visited today. These walls of earth recall the description of the old town in the *Book of Rights* as 'embanked Dublin'.

Though findings from the earliest eras of the Castle were meagre, substantial structures from the medieval period of its history were recovered.

At the south-west corner, close to the Bermingham Tower, part of the curtain wall from the earliest Norman period was found. This had been incorporated into the thirteenth-century wall running between the Bermingham Tower and the Cork Tower. The Bermingham Tower was, of course, rebuilt during the eighteenth century, and is now in use as part of the State Apartments. The archaeologists found the foundations of a square tower projecting from its base, which had been reduced in the seventeenth century and had possibly been used as a gun platform.

The Cork Tower had collapsed in 1624 and had then been rebuilt, and the base of this tower survived to a height of five metres underneath the eighteenth-century west cross Block. This was exposed as a feature outside the Conference Centre. The reinforcing cross timbers which had been built into the tower were found

however, it was cut through boulder clay. The town walls met the Castle walls over arches which allowed the free flow of water and access for small boats. Though landing steps were found at the Powder Tower, these arches had been blocked up for security in the fourteenth century, the moat then being filled (as it is today) by natural springs.

Over the centuries the moat made a convenient dumping place. The sewage from the Castle garderobes flowed into it as well. Little effort was made to scour it, and over time it filled up, was lined by trees and then finally built over from the town side, reducing its width by half. Eventually an alleyway, Cole's Alley, was laid along it, linking Ship Street with Castle Street. Here houses were built in the early eighteenth century facing onto Cole's Alley and Silver Court. However, after Emmet's Rising in 1803 the government bought up the houses (which had become occupied by silk-dyers, wigmakers, metal smiths, surgeons and lawyers). The houses were torn down to ground level and the impressive panelled wall described earlier was erected.

In the course of these 'highly successful' excavations some 10,000 artefacts were found. These ranged in date from Viking times up to the eighteenth century. As in all digs, ceramics and pottery were found in abundance, some imports from France and England, others locally made. Others came from China, Germany, Holland, Spain, Portugal, France and England. In the moat were found leather shoes, scabbards, clothes, coins, tokens, keys, buckles pins, needles, knives, lace-point, arrows, spear heads and spats. Bone items, mostly from the Viking period, were especially plentiful, together with glasses and bottles from the seventeenth and eighteenth centuries.

The foundations of the Powder Tower, part of the city wall, a water gate and a postern door with steps leading down to a small jetty were left permanently uncovered. Today this undercroft can been seen by visitors, and is an eerie contact with the earliest days of the Castle for, of course, the foundations of the tower belonged to the first part of the work on the Norman structure in 1204.

LEFT: *The foundations of the Powder Tower, now open to visitors, one of the most dramatic if eerie sights on the Dublin Castle tour*
AN DÚCHAS THE HERITAGE SERVICE

perfectly preserved because of the waterlogged condition of the site.

The most impressive finds were those which are open to the visitor today at the Powder Tower on the north-eastern corner of the Castle. Here almost the full outline of the round tower was found underlying the eighteenth-century erections. When the excavations were complete it rose to a height of six metres, and enclosed within it layers of Viking material.

The medieval gateway to the Castle lay under what is now the Bedford Tower. Here excavations revealed the causeway crossing the moat to the main gate, through which Sir Henry Sidney is shown riding in John Derricke's woodcut. Massive foundations for walls on both sides of the causeway seem to have been the remains of a barbican, and there was a space to take a drawbridge halfway across. A second drawbridge may have crossed the ditch which was uncovered at the outer entrance to the barbican. All of these finds indicated just how well the medieval Castle had been defended.

The Castle was surrounded in medieval times by a moat, through which water from the Poddle flowed, and the moat was a minor part of these excavations. It averaged 20–22 metres in width and was cut 8–9 metres deep into the underlying limestone. At the Cork Tower,

* * *

141

The Minister of State for Arts and Culture

and Mrs. Kitt

request the pleasure of your company

at a Reception

in the State Apartments, Dublin Castle

on Monday, 15 June, 1992

at 8.00 p.m.

on the occasion of the XIII International

Joyce Symposium

RIGHT: *Official invitation to the Dublin Castle State Reception to mark the Centenary of the birth of James Joyce in 1982*

Typical of the events which were held in the restored Castle was the state reception for the centenary of James Joyce, an event to which were invited such distinguished guests as Anthony Burgess and Jorge Luis Borges. Here the great and the good of modern Ireland mingled with the varied guests from many countries who had come to Ireland to honour an author once thought of as being beyond the pale. It was a firm indication of the ever-changing nature of Ireland.

The plans for Ireland's second European Presidency in 1990 involved the creation of a purpose-built Conference Centre in one part of the site, along with major work elsewhere. By December 1989: the restoration work on the Castle was completed by the Office of Public Works just in time for 1 January. The Chapel Royal, whose foundations had been strengthened to prevent it from sinking into the Poddle below, re-opened on New Year's Day with a choral recital. The wonderful internal plasterwork by George Stapleton was restored and the wood carving by Richard Stewart cleaned. The stained glass depicting the Passion of Christ which fills the four central panels of the east window had been presented to the chapel by Lord Whitworth, who bought it on a tour of the Continent. Though the old communion table has been restored, the

Stations of the Cross (carved by the monks at Glenstal) have been retained from its Catholic period. It is now no longer used for any kind of religious service, which seems a pity. The ecumenical service of prayers for the opening of every new Dáil are now held in St Patrick's Hall, a setting in which the Chief Rabbi and the Imam of Dublin, representing respectively the Jewish and Muslim communities in Ireland, feel free to attend.

The blind gate to the west of the Bedford Tower was now opened, and a new arching bridge across the revealed moat gave a new access point. The arcade of the former La Touche Bank was incorporated into a walkway connecting the new Castle Hall behind the Bedford Tower with the Conference Centre. The additions to the Tower were removed, restoring it to its original appearance. The courtyard too was re-cobbled as it would have been in the early Victorian period.

Ship Street Barracks was renovated as offices. Leitrim House, the old Ordnance Office, was now restored and extended, with a covered-in walk way to create museum space. The Coach House was also renovated as part of the reception areas. The elegant castellated façade of this building is often said to have been erected to screen the sensitive eyes of Queen Victoria from the backs of the houses to the south – it clearly appears in the Ordnance Survey map of 1843.

The new facilities provided space not only for state receptions, but also for media events like the extended inquiry into the Irish meat industry. The Beef Tribunal grew into the most expensive and extended inquiry in the history of the state, although it was perhaps surpassed by the more recent inquiry into the Dunnes' payments to politicians at which the reclusive Mr Charles Haughey was finally brought to give humiliating evidence.

Once again in 1996 Ireland held the Presidency of the European Union. On this occasion more work was put in hand. The garden to the rear of the Castle was laid out, the old coach house was converted to a small reception and exhibition area, and Leitrim House, where the Telephones Section of the old Posts and Telegraphs had once been housed, was now restored as the Clock Tower House. This had originally been the officers' quarters of the Ship Street Barracks. The courtyard was roofed over with glass and a new extension added to the rear to house the Chester Beatty Library collections.

The former barracks lying to the rear of the Castle along Ship Street were finally saved and restored as offices for various smaller government departments.

As it appeared on newscasts beamed worldwide, Dublin Castle appeared as fine a presence as any historic site in Europe or America.

The centre provides a range of facilities, from the great Conference Hall which can hold up to five hundred persons for a reception down to a room which will provide a boardroom for as few as twenty. These are all situated in the old west range and in the reconverted Bedford Tower, to which a new hall has been added by incorporating the old La Touche Bank building.

At the heart of these is the Moat Pool, overlooked by dining and bar areas. The walls of the rooms are hung not only with paintings from the Castle's historic past (including a portrait of Lord Aberdeen), but also with works by modern Irish artists. The catering and technical facilities reach the highest of international standards; and in fact Dublin Castle is a member of the prestigious Historic Conference Centres of Europe. The Coach House is now part of the same centre This building was erected at the time of Queen Victoria's visit to Ireland, to house the viceregal horses and coaches, though the neo-gothic façade facing the gardens suggests an altogether grander use.

Increasingly at the centre of a wide variety of activities, Dublin Castle today also houses not only small theatre groups using the Crypt Art Space, but also *Poetry Ireland*, Music Network, Gaisce, *The Irish Arts Review*, Amharclann de hIde, and An Taisce (the National Trust for Ireland).

LEFT: *The figures of Agriculture and Industry by John Hughes, from the Queen Victoria memorial, now in the roof garden*

Busy as it is today, Dublin Castle also has its quiet place. On our walk around the Castle confines, we could also have gone up the steps just inside the back gate of the Castle which would have led into a raised garden decorated with some of the figures by John Hughes RHA which graced the foot of the great statue of Queen Victoria which once stood before Leinster House before its removal in 1948. These show a wounded Irish soldier cared for by Hibernia, and the figures of Plenty, and of Industry. They are the strangely moving fragments of a great Irish artist's most famous work. The Queen herself (after years of neglect) has been 'sent to Botany Bay' and now graces the city of Victoria in Australia. Descending from this garden in the sky, an archway would have let us out through the Corke Tower into the Upper Castle Yard.

Standing in the Upper Castle Yard, we are looking at the last use of brick on a grand scale in the public buildings of Georgian Dublin, work which was completed round 1750. '*The total effect,*' Maurice Craig wrote half a century ago, '*in redbrick with cream stone trimmings, segment-headed ground-floor windows and arcades at salient points, is charming in intimate collegiate fashion, persuading one to forget the evil role of the Castle in Irish affairs. Upper Castle Yard, in particular, evokes to perfection complacent Hanoverian corruption of that era. It seems to tell us that though every man has his price, the prices are moderate and have all been paid on the nail. Everything is running like well oiled clockwork, and the clockwork soldiers are changing guard in front of the Bedford Tower.'*

This evokes a scene like the one which the Rev. Calvert Jones photographed in 1846.

But, though times change, human nature stays much the same. It was in this same square that a great crowd gathered in the summer of 1997 to witness the triumphant departure of Mr Charles Haughey after his humiliation before the Dunnes' Payments tribunal. Every man may still have his price, and it is an indication of how successful modern Ireland has become that that price, still paid on the nail, has risen to a million pounds.

It is here that, day by day, other tribunals of the people resolutely expose the venalities of the current moment. These tribunals are a return to an ancient use of the Castle, and undoubtedly in the future this square will be the setting for other, even more extraordinary scenes. Here Irish history continues to be made.

THE STATE
APARTMENTS

WHAT THE VISITOR CAN SEE TODAY

Having returned to the Upper Castle Yard, we can now turn into the State Apartments, which is what most visitors today wish to see, and take up our tour where we left it after our circuit of the Castle confines.

Battleaxe Landing

After leaving the outer and inner hallways, we now climb a staircase which divides to the left and right to reach Battleaxe Landing. Today there are no weapons on view: the name comes from the old days when the armed guards of the Viceroys would have been stationed along the walls. The carpets here and throughout the Castle were specially woven at Killybegs, under the direction of Raymond McGrath when he undertook the first large-scale refurbishment of the Castle for the Board of Works in the 1940s. The chandeliers are also Irish, made in Waterford.

On the walls of the stair-well are displayed the coats of arms of the Presidents of Ireland since 1937, complemented by the arms of Ireland over the central doorway at the top.

The tapestries are from the Gobelins factory in France and are eighteenth century, while the tables are topped with Italian marble.

The James Connolly Room

On turning to the right on the landing, we enter the east wing of the State Apartments. This part of the Castle was completely reconstructed in 1960s, though the guide does not allude to this. The rooms were, however, largely restored to follow the layout and appearance of the original state bedrooms used to entertain visitors in the past. A corridor, closed to visitors, leads to the Middle Tower, from which a small footbridge connects with the Castle Garden.

The first bedroom contains a memorial plaque to the socialist James Connolly, the leader of the Irish Citizen Army, which joined the Irish Volunteers in the Easter Rising in 1916. Having been badly wounded during the fighting, he was brought here for treatment after the GPO surrendered, and was confined in a room on this site until he was taken 'sitting in a chair' to Kilmainham Gaol for execution.

The Granard Room

Also a former state bedroom, this room contains items donated to the Castle by the Earl of Granard in memory of his mother, Beatrice Countess of Granard, and her husband the 8th Earl of Granard (who died in 1948). The ceiling is one of those items which were removed from Sarah Purser's home, Mespil House, before it was demolished by developers in the 1950s. It is thought to show Hibernia herself.

The King's Bedroom

The largest of these rooms, it was here that Kings Edward VII and George V slept on their visits to Ireland. The attractive mahogany table here was formerly in St George's Hall and was once the property of Lord Norbury, the notorious 'Hanging Judge' who sentenced Robert Emmet. It was actually decorated by a prisoner in gaol using small pieces of veneer that came his way.

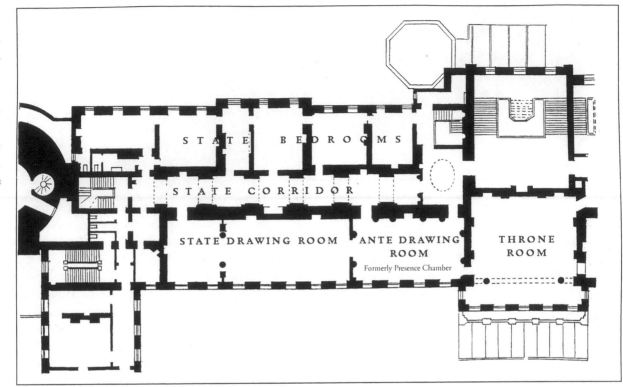

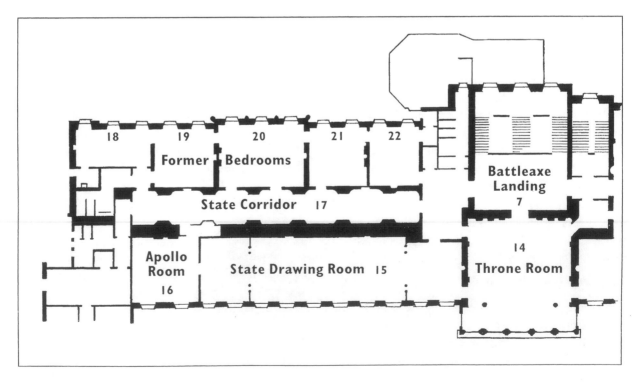

On the mantelpiece are French clocks and Italian statues, while the painting, 'The Sacrifice of Isaac' is by the Dutch artist Devos.

The *Arts and Sciences* Room

The ceiling here, which shows representations of 'The Arts and Sciences' was also removed from Mespil House. The Sheraton furniture is intended to complement the eighteenth-century setting.

The Queen's Bedroom

In continuity with the previous room, the furniture here is Regency, though the chandelier is from Limoges. Like the King's Bedroom, it has three windows, which overlook the Castle Garden.

The State Corridor

The original corridor was thought to have been the work of Edward Lovett Pearce (1699–1733), who did much work on the Castle, though his most memorable building is the Parliament House (now the Bank of Ireland) in College Green. The five rooms off the corridors were once used as bedrooms for state visitors.

The Apollo Room

During the reconstruction of this wing (1964–8), an opportunity was taken to instal here the back drawing room from Tracton House, on the corner of St Stephen's Green and Merrion Row, beside the old Huguenot cemetery. Though the timber panelling is a copy, the ceiling and the mantelpiece are original.

The ceiling shows Apollo, resting with his lyre on clouds surrounded by the signs of the Zodiac. The corner pieces are intended to represent hunting, war, agriculture and music. It is dated 1746 but the artist is unknown.

The State Drawing Room

This was the room where the fire broke out in 1941. It was then reconstructed by Raymond McGrath, in an eighteenth-century French style. Though the chandeliers of Waterford glass were new, the rest of the decoration was carefully restored (the chimney glasses, the pier glasses and the console tables). The paintings, part of the Milltown Gift in the National Gallery, are by Giovanni Paolo Panini, an artist who specialised in picturesque ruins. It was here, on 31 November 1997, that Mary McAleese received the notification of her election to the supreme office of President from an army officer of the Presidential staff.

The Throne Room

This room is also known as the Presence Chamber. The throne which graces it is said to have been cut down to accommodate Queen Victoria, a very small woman, on her first visit to Ireland at the time of the Famine. It dates from the seventeenth century and was presented to the Castle by William III when he seized the throne of England. The brass chandelier of Dublin workmanship dates from the time of the Act of Union in 1801. The Throne Room was last used for an official purpose during the state visit to Ireland of George V and Queen Mary in 1911. The four roundels show Jupiter, Juno, Mars and Venus, though the subjects of the two ovals are unindentified. All are the work of Giambattista Bellucci, the eighteenth-century Venetian artist.

Picture Gallery

On leaving the Throne Room, we enter the west wing and the Picture Gallery, which runs parallel to St Patrick's Hall. This was once three rooms (divided where the Doric columns now stand): the central room was the State Dining Room and the smaller rooms were the Drawing Room and Small Dining Room. The Gallery is now hung with portraits of the Viceroys, including Lord Cornwallis of American Revolution fame.

The Wedgwood Room

This charming little room was used as a billiard room in the nineteenth century. The Wedgwood plaques are the work of John Flaxman, the circular plaques are reproductions of 'Night' and 'Day' by Berthal Thorwaldson, and the three ceiling paintings are by Angelica Kaufmann, who visited Ireland as the guest of the Viceroy Lord Townshend in 1717.

147

The Bermingham Tower Room

Reached from the previous room, as well as from St Patrick's Hall, this tower is an echo of the medieval Castle, for it stands on the site of one of the original bastions. It was formerly used as a prison and as a store for papers, but it was damaged by an explosion in the powder magazine in 1775. Two years later it was completely rebuilt in less heavy materials, and was then used as a supper room. The nineteenth-century brass chandelier incorporates the entwined symbols of England, Ireland and Scotland – the Rose, Shamrock and Thistle – and this theme is repeated in the carpet.

St Patrick's Hall

This room is the real centrepiece of the Castle. It takes its name from the Order of St Patrick instituted in 1783. The banners are those of the Knights of the Order in 1922 (after which, as we have seen, only a handful were added).

The ceiling paintings are by Vincenzo Valdre. In chronological order they show: St Patrick lighting the Paschal fire on the Hill of Slane in 433; Henry II receiving the submission of the Irish kings in 1171; and (in the centre) George III with the figures of Liberty and Justice.

The gallery above the main entrance was used once for visitors, and the second gallery for musicians. The busts are of the Duke of Wellington, and of Lord Chesterfield, who is thought to have first suggested the erection of the hall in 1746.

RIGHT: *The banners of the Knights of St Patrick still hang in a place of honour in the Castle*

The stall plates along the walls are arranged in chronological order, as they stood in 1922. The banners are the Royal Standard, and the personal banners of the following knights:

Viscount Powerscourt
Earl of Mayo
Earl of Meath
Earl of Shaftesbury
Earl of Desart
Earl of Granard
Viscount Pirrie
Baron Oranmore and Browne
Earl of Enniskillen
Royal Standard
Earl of Listowel
Viscount French of Ypres
Duke of Abercorn
Baron Monteagle of Brandon
Earl of Donoughmore
Earl of Arran
Earl Castletown
Earl of Brandon
Earl of Dunraven
Earl of Iveagh
Earl of Midleton
Earl of Cavan

Double doors lead back onto the landing of the Battleaxe Stair, and so back to the front hall and the entrance to the Upper Castle Yard.

Some rooms which were formerly on show are no longer part of the public tour of the Castle. These are: the Guardroom (McKee–Clancy–Clune memorial), Ante-Room, and St George's Hall.

The former Guardroom was opened by the de Valera Government in the 1930s as a memorial to Dick McKee and his colleages, whose death has already been described. The house in Exchange Court has been sold and the room can no longer be seen by the public, a reversal of history which has dismayed many Republicans. A plaque, erected by the National Graves Association, can still be read on the outside wall.

In the Ante-Room (reached from the Picture Gallery) was formerly displayed a Waterford crystal service made for President O'Kelly. A painting which then hung here was supposed to show the Battle of the Boyne. There was also a curious inscription on the back of the portrait of Lord Chesterfield that also hung here and had once belonged to the famous 'dangerous papist' Miss Ambrose, who was thought by ill-disposed Protestants to exert too much influence over the Viceroy. She prized the picture highly, but fell on hard times, dying in poverty in her Eccles Street home in 1814. She had willed the painting to the Castle, but when it arrived the Viceroy of the day was not in residence and there was no one to take responsibility for it. It was moved about from wall to wall, and room to room, until in 1870 it was identified after a valet had complained that he did not like having it in his room as it was so dark and dirty that it was impossible to tell whether the figure was a man or a woman.

St George's Hall was built in 1911 for the state visit of the newly-crowned George V and Queen Mary, the last royal visit to Dublin, when they opened the College of Science (now Government Buildings) in Upper Merrion Street. It was furnished with paintings by the Flemish artist Peter de Gree, and a table said to have belonged to Lord Norbury, which are now elsewhere in the State Apartments.

This room has been converted for public use, as mentioned earlier, and it is here that the Tribunals of Inquiry now sit. It forms part of the Dublin Castle Conference Centre, which emerged from the most recent renovations of the fabric of the Castle.

The Chapel Royal and the Wardrobe Tower

ENVOI

With the completion of the renovation in 1996, the Castle, which had been shabby and neglected a generation before, was given a completely new lease of life.

This local renewal was a reflection of a wider sense of national well-being. Symbolic of this was the inauguration in St Patrick's Hall in November 1997 of the eighth President of Ireland, Mary MacAleese, as successor to the popular seventh president Mary Robinson.

In a break with custom, Mrs MacAleese moved afterwards among the great crowd of well-wishers in the Upper Yard, shaking hands with young and old. What a contrast this scene made with former days.

Ireland's emergence as the 'Celtic Tiger', and as one of the leading holiday destinations in Europe for weekenders, together with its hosting of the European presidency, marked the great distance which the March of the Nation has covered in a century.

The installation of Mrs MacAleese's successors will symbolise the new continuity of past and present now represented by the Castle, as a new century and a new millennium approach. How appropriate, then, that it was here that the settlement of the future of Ireland as a whole was decided in the spring of 1998, when the returning officer announced in both Gaelic and Irish (if we can now so term the language of the majority of people in Ireland) a 98 per cent approval by the electorate of the terms of the Good Friday settlement. For the first time since that distant election in 1918, the whole of Ireland had been polled on the same day on the same issue. Here, all were agreed, there was a new beginning in Irish history, a new beginning witnessed in Dublin Castle.

Perhaps only today, approaching the end of the twentieth century, after its long and eventful history over two thousand years or more, has Dublin Castle become fully re-integrated into the life of the Irish nation.

Lords Lieutenant and Lords Deputy of Ireland

1172	Hugh de Lacy
1173	Richard, Earl of Pembroke
1176	Raymond le Gros
1177	Prince John
1203	Hugh de Lacy
1199	Meyler FitzHenry
1203	Hugh de Lacy
1204	Meyler FitzHenry
1205	Hugh de Lacy
1215	Geoffrey de Marisco
1308	Piers Gaveston
1312	Edmund le Botiller
1316	Roger de Mortimer
1320	Thomas Fitzgerald
1321	John de Bermingham
1327	Earl of Kildare
1328	Prior Roger Outlow
1332	Sir John d'Arcy
1337	Sir John de Cherlton
1340	Prior Roger Outlow
1344	Sir Raoul de Ufford
1346	Sir Roger d'Arcy
	Sir John Moriz
1348	Walter de Bermingham
1355	Maurice, Earl of Desmond
1356	Thomas de Rokeby
1357	Almaric de St Amand
1359	James, Earl of Ormonde
1361	Lionel, Duke of Clarence
1367	Gerald, Earl of Desmond
1369	William de Windsor
1376	Maurice, Earl of Desmond
	James, Earl of Ormonde
1380	Edmund Mortimer, Earl of March
1385	Robert de Vere, Earl of Oxford
1389	Sir John Stanley
1391	James, Earl of Ormonde
1393	Thomas, Duke of Gloucester
1395	Roger de Mortimer, Lord Justice
	Reginald Grey, Lord Justice
1398	Thomas de Holland
1398	Sir John Stanley

1401	Thomas, Earl of Lancaster
	Sir John Stanley
1413	Sir John Talbot
1420	James, Earl of Ormonde
1423	Edmund de Mortimer, Earl of March
1425	Sir John Talbot
1427	Sir John Grey
1428	Sir John Sutton
1431	Sir Thomas Stanley
1438	Lionel, Lord de Wells
1446	John Talbot, Earl of Shrewsbury
1449	Richard, Duke of York
1461	George, Duke of Clarence
1470	John Tiptoft, Earl of Worcester
1472	George, Duke of Clarence (again)
1478	John de la Pole, Earl of Suffolk
1483	Gerald, Earl of Kildare
1484	John de la Pole, Earl of Lincoln
1488	Jasper Tudor, Duke of Bedford
1494	Henry, Duke of York (afterwards Henry VIII)
1496	Gerald, Earl of Kildare
1521	Thomas Howard, Earl of Surrey
1529	Henry, Duke of Richmond
1560	Thomas, Earl of Sussex
1599	Robert, Earl of Essex
1603	Charles Blount, Lord Mountjoy
1622	Henry Carey, Viscount Falkland
1629	Thomas Wentworth, Earl of Strafford
1643	James, Marquess of Ormonde
1647	Philip, Lord Lisle
1649	Oliver Cromwell
1657	Henry Cromwell
1662	James, Duke of Ormonde
1669	John, Lord Robartes
1670	John, Lord Berkeley of Stratton
1672	Arthur, Earl of Essex
1677	James, Duke of Ormonde
1685	Henry Hyde, Earl of Clarendon
1687	Richard Talbot, Earl of Tyrconnel
1692	Henry, Viscount Sydney of Shepey
1695	Henry, Lord Capell of Tewkesbury
1700	Laurence Hyde, Earl of Rochester
1703	James, Duke of Ormonde

1707	Thomas, Duke of Pembroke	1830	Marquess of Anglesey (again)
1709	Thomas, Earl of Wharton	1833	Richard, Marquess Wellesley
1710	Thomas, Duke of Ormonde	1834	Thomas Hamilton, Earl of Haddington
1713	Charles, Duke of Shrewsbury	1835	Constantine Phipps, Viscount, afterwards Marquess, of Normanby
1717	Charles Powlett, Duke of Bolton		
1721	Charles FitzRoy, Duke of Grafton	1839	Hugh, Lord, afterwards Earl, Fortescue
1724	John, Lord Carteret	1841	Thomas Philip, Earl de Grey
1731	Lionel Sackville, Duke of Dorset	1844	William A'Court, Lord Heytesbury
1737	William Cavendish, Duke of Devonshire	1846	John William Ponsonby, Earl of Bessborough
1745	Philip Dormer Stanhope, Earl of Chesterfield	1847	George Villiers, Earl of Clarendon
1746	William Stanhope, Earl of Harrington	1852	Archibald William Montgomerie, Earl of Eglinton
1751	Duke of Dorset (again)		
1755	William Cavendish, fourth Duke of Devonshire	1853	Edward Granville Eliot, Earl of St Germans
1756	John Russell, Duke of Bedford	1855	George William Frederick Howard, Earl of Carlisle
1761	George Montague, Earl of Halifax		
1763	Hugh Smithson, Earl of Northumberland	1858	Earl of Eglinton (again)
1765	Francis SeymourConway, Earl of Hertford	1859	Earl of Carlisle (again)
1767	George, Viscount Townshend	1864	John, Lord Wodehouse (Earl of Kimberley)
1772	Simon, Earl Harcourt	1866	James Hamilton, Marquess of Abercorn
1777	John Hobart, Earl of Buckinghamshire	1868	John, Earl Spencer
1780	Frederick Howard, Earl of Carlisle	1874	James, Duke (formerly Marquess) of Abercorn
1782	William Henry Cavendish-Bentinck, Duke of Portland	1876	John Winston Spencer Churchill, Duke of Marlborough
	George Grenville, Earl Temple	1880	Francis, Earl Cowper
1783	Robert Henley, Earl of Northington	1882	Earl Spencer (again)
1784	Charles Manners, Duke of Rutland	1885	Henry Herbert, Earl of Carnarvon
1787	Marquess of Buckingham (the Earl Temple, appointed 1782)	1886	John Campbell Hamilton Gordon, Earl of Aberdeen
1790	John Fane, Earl of Westmorland	1886	Charles Stewart Vane Tempest, Marquess of Londonderry
1795	William, Earl Fitzwilliam		
	John Pratt, Earl Camden	1889	Lawrence Dundas, Earl of Zetland
1798	Charles, Marquess Cornwallis	1892	Robert Offley Ashburton Milnes, Lord Houghton (afterwards Earl of Crewe)
1801	Philip Yorke, Earl of Hardwicke		
1806	John Russell, Duke of Bedford	1895	George Henry, Earl Cadogan
1807	Charles Lennox, Duke of Richmond	1902	William Humble Ward, Earl of Dudley
1813	Charles, Viscount, afterwards Earl, Whitworth	1905	Earl of Aberdeen (again)
1817	Charles, Earl Talbot	1915	Ivor Churchill Guest, Lord, afterwards Viscount, Wimborne
1821	Richard, Marquess Wellesley		
1828	Henry William Paget, Marquess of Anglesey	1918	John, Viscount French of Ypres
1829	Hugh Percy, Duke of Northumberland	1921	Edmund, Viscount FitzAlan

BIBLIOGRAPHY

This list includes not only the immediate sources for this account of Dublin Castle's complicated history, but also some material on the general history of Dublin and Ireland, which may be of use to readers wishing to follow up some particular aspect of the story.

Alcock, Leslie. *Arthur's Britain: History and Archaeology AD 367–634*. London, 1971.

Anstruther, Ian. *The Knight and the Umbrella: An Account of the Eglinton Tournament 1839*. London, 1963.

Bamford, Francis, and Viola Bankes. *Vicious Circle*. London, 1965.

Barnard, Francis Pierrepont. *Strongbow's Conquest of Ireland 1166–1186* (English History from Contemporary Writers). London, 1883.

Barry, T.B. *The Archaeology of Medieval Ireland*. London and New York, 1987

Bayley, W.J., *Historical Sketches of the Castle*. Dublin, n.d.

Beatha Aodha Ruaidh Uí Dhomhnaill. *Transcribed from the Book of Lughaidh ó Clérigh with introduction and notes by Rev. Paul Walsh*. Dublin, 1948, pp.11–21.

Bell, J. Bowyer. *The Secret Army: A History of the IRA 1916–1970*. London, 1970.

Bence-Jones, Mark. *Twilight of the Ascendancy*. London, 1987.

Bennett, Douglas. *Encyclopedia of Dublin*. Dublin, 1991.

Bethell, Denis. 'Norman Origins,' *Ireland of the Welcomes*, 18, 1, May-June 1969, pp.21–27.

Bewley, Charles. *Memoirs of a Wild Goose*. Dublin, c.1994.

Bradley, John. ed. *Viking Dublin Exposed*. Dublin, 1984.

—— 'The Topographical Development of Scandinavian Dublin,' in *Dublin City and County: From Prehistory to the Present*, ed. F.H.A. Aalen and Kevin Whelan. Dublin, 1992.

Broad, Ian and Bride Roseny. *Medieval Dublin: Two Historic Walks*. Dublin, 1982.

Buckland, Gail. *Fox Talbot and the Invention of Photography*. London, 1980.

Casey, Michael. 'The Most Illustrious Order of St. Patrick,' *Dublin Historical Record*, XLIV (2), Autumn 1991, 4–12.

Chambers, Anne. *Eleanor, Countess of Desmond: A Heroine of Tudor Ireland*. Dublin, 1986.

Chart, D.A. *The Story of Dublin*. London, 1932

Clarke, D. *Dublin*. London, 1977.

Clarke, Howard B. 'The Topographical Development of Early Modern Dublin,' *JRSAI*, 107 (1977), 29–51.

—— *Dublin c.840–c.1450: The Medieval Town in the Modern City*. Map prepared for the Friends of Medieval Dublin and the Ordnance Survey of Ireland, 1978.

—— ed. *Medieval Dublin: The Making of a Metropolis*. Dublin, 1990.

—— ed. *Medieval Dublin: The Living City*. Dublin, 1990.

Conlin, Stephen. *Historic Dublin*. Dublin, 1986.

Cornford, John: 'Dublin Castle', *Country Life*, 3823 (30 July 1970); 3824 (6 August 1970); 3826 (20 August 1970).

Corr, Marie. 'Digging against the clock,' *Irish Times*, 23 January 1986.

Caisleán Bhaile Átha Cliath. Dublin Castle (with drawings by D. Newman Johnson). Dublin, n.d. [c.1965]

Craig, Maurice James. *Dublin 1660–1800*. London, 1952.

Culliton, J. *The City Hall*. Dublin, 1982.

Curran, C.P. *Dublin Plasterwork*. London, 1965.

Curtis, Edmund. *A History of Ireland*. London, 1936.

Dalton, Charles. *With the Dublin Brigade*. London, 1929.

D'Alton, J. *The History of the County of Dublin*. Dublin, 1838.

de Brefny, Brian. *Castle of Ireland*. London, 1979.

de Courcy, J.W. *The Liffey in Dublin*. Dublin, 1996.

de Paor, Liam. 'Fighting Men,' *Ireland of the Welcomes*, 18, 1, May-June 1969, 32–35.

Derricke, John. *The Image of Irelande*. London, 1581 (new editions Edinburgh, 1883; Belfast, 1984).

Dolly, Michael. 'The Normans – A Lasting Impact,' *Ireland of the Welcomes*, 18, 1, May-June 1969, 36–39.

Duggan, C.G. 'The Last Days of Dublin Castle,' *Blackwood's Magazine*, Vol.212, August 1922, 137–190.

Dunne, John J. 'Place of Quiet Prayer in Heart of Dublin City.' *Irish Catholic*, 19 September 1985.

Edward, R. Dudley and T.D. Williams (eds). *The Great Famine*. Dublin, 1956.

Faulkner, Caesar Litton. *Illustrations of Irish History and Topography*. London, 1904.

—— *Essays Relating to Ireland*. London, 1909.

F.E.R. *Historical Reminiscences of Dublin Castle from 849 to 1904*. Dublin, 1904.

Finegan, Francis. 'Irish Confessors and Martyrs', *The New Catholic Encyclopedia*. New York, 1956.

Fingall, Elizabeth Plunkett, Countess of. *Seventy Years Young*. London, 1937.

Fitzpatrick, Samuel A. Ossory. *Dublin: A Historical and Topographical Account of the City*. London, 1907.

Galloway, Peter. *The Most Illustrious Order of St. Patrick*. London, 1983.

Gilbert, J.T. *History of Dublin*. Dublin, 1854–59.

—— *History of the Viceroys of Ireland; with Notices of the Castle of Dublin and its Chief Occupants in Former Times*. Dublin, 1865.

Gilbert, J.T and R.M. Gilbert (eds). *Calendar of Ancient Records of Dublin in Possession of the Municipal Corporation of that City*. Dublin, 1889–1944.

Gill and Son (ed). *Guide to Catholic Dublin*. Dublin, 1932.

Gillespie, Elgy (ed). *The Liberties of Dublin*. Dublin, 1973.

Giraldus Cambrensis. *Expugnatio Hibernica: The Conquest of Ireland by Giraldus Cambrensis*. Edited and translated by A.B. Scott and F.X. Martin. Dublin, 1978.

Gorham, Maurice. *Dublin from Old Photographs*. London, 1972.

Gould, Rupert T. 'Abraham Thornton Offers Battle,' in *Enigmas*. London, 1946.

Graham-Campbell, J. '1976 'The Viking-age Silver Hoards of Ireland', in Almquist, B. and Greene, D. (eds) *Proceedings of the Seventh Viking Congress*, Dublin 1976.

Haliday, Charles. *The Scandinavia Kingdom of Dublin*. Dublin, 1881; 2nd ed. 1884.

Handbook to the City of Dublin and the Surrounding District, prepared for the meeting of the British Association, September 1908. Dublin, 1908.

Harris, Walter. *The History and Antiquities of the City of Dublin*. Dublin, 1776.

Harvey, John. *Dublin: A Study in Environment.* London, 1948.

Hayes-McCoy, G.A. (ed). *The Irish at War.* Cork, 1964.

Hollinshed, Raphael. *Second Volume of Chronicles First Collected by Raphael Hollinshed, now Newlie Recognised Augmented and Continued by John Hooke, alias Vowell.* London, 1586.

Hone, J.M. *The Life of George Moore.* London, 1936.

Hughes, L.J. 'Dublin Castle in the Seventeenth Century,' *Dublin Historical Record*, 2, 1940, 81–97.

Landreth, Helen. *The Pursuit of Robert Emmet.* Dublin, 1949.

Larkin, Emmet. *James Larkin.* London, 1965.

Lawlor, Rev. H.J. 'The Chapel of Dublin Castle,' *JRSAI* 13, 1923, 49–51.

Leask, Harold G. *Caisleán Bhaile Átha Cliath; Dublin Castle. A Short Description and Historical Guide for the Use of Visitors.* Dublin, n.d. (*c.*1944).

—— *Irish Castles and Castellated Houses.* Dundalk, 1944.

Lennon, Colm. *The Lords of Dublin in the Age of Reformation.* Dublin, 1989.

—— 'Dublin's Great Explosion of 1597,' *History Ireland*, 3, 3, Autumn 1995, 29–34.

Lewis, Richard. *The Dublin Guide.* Dublin, 1787.

Little, George A. *Dublin before the Vikings: An Adventure in Discovery.* Dublin, 1957.

Loeber, Rolf. 'The Rebuilding of Dublin Castle: Thirty Critical years, 1661–1690,' *Studies*, 69, 1980, 45–69

Lynch, Ann, and Conleth Manning 'Dublin Castle. The Archaeological Project,' *Archaeology Ireland*, 4(2), 1990, 65–8.

McBride, Laurence W. *The Greening of the Castle.* Washington DC, 1992.

Macardle, Dorothy. *The Irish Republic.* 5th revised ed.Dublin, 1999.

McDonald, Frank. 'Dublin Castle Abandoned – "Would the British let the Tower Fall Down?"' *Irish Times*, 9 August 1983.

—— 'Dublin Castle's Right Royal Masterpeice.' *Irish Times*, 17 August 1991.

MacLysaght, Edward. *Irish Life in the Seventeenth Century.* Dublin, 1979.

MacNeill, Eoin. 'Where does Irish History Begin?' *The New Ireland Review*, 1906, 1–17.

MacNiffe, Liam. *A History of the Garda Síochána.* Dublin, 1996.

Maguire, J.B. *Dublin Castle: Historical Background and Guide.* Dublin, 1970.

—— 'Seventeenth Century Plans of Dublin Castle' *JRSAI* 104, 1974, 5–14.

—— 'Dublin Castle: Three Centuries of Development' *JRSAI* 115, 1985, 13–39.

Malton, James. *A Picturesque and Descriptive View of the City of Dublin.* London, 1794.

Markham, Thomas. [Article on the death of Clune, Clancy and McKee]. *Irish Independent*, 12 October, 1932.

Maxwell, Constantia. *Dublin under the Georges, 1714–1830.* London, 1936.

Mills, John FitzMaurice. *The Noble Dwellings of Ireland.* London, 1987.

Moody, T.W., F.X. Martin, F.J. Byrne (eds). *A Chronology of Irish History* [companion to *New Oxford History of Ireland*]. London, 1982.

Moore, George. *A Drama in Muslin.* London, 1886; Belfast, 1992.

—— *Parnell and His Island.* London, 1887.

Murphy, Denis. *Our Martyrs.* Dublin, 1896.

National Museum of Ireland. *Viking and Medieval Dublin: National Museum Excavations 1962–1973.* Dublin, 1973.

Neligan, David. *A Spy in the Castle.* London,1968.

O'Brien, Richard Barry. *Dublin Castle and the Irish People.* London, 1912.

Ó'Broin, Leon. *Dublin Castle and the 1916 Rising.* Dublin, 1966.

—— *The Prime Informer: A Suppressed Scandal.* London, 1971.

O'Donnell, E.E. *The Annals of Dublin – Fair City.* Dublin, 1988.

O'Donovan, Donal. *God's Architect: A Life of Raymond McGrath.* Bray, 1995.

O'Donovan, John (ed). *The Annals of the Kingdom of Ireland by the Four Masters.* Dublin, 1848–1851.

O'Duffy, Eimar. *The Wasted Island.* Dublin, 1920.

O'Dwyer, Frederick. *Lost Dublin.* Dublin, 1981.

Official Guide to Dublin, Dublin, 1928.

O'Kelly, M.J. *Newgrange.* London, 1982.

Ó Lochlainn, Colm. 'Roadways in Ancient Ireland,' in John Ryan (ed.), *Essays and Studies Presented to Professor Eoin MacNeill on the Occasion of his Seventieth Birthday, 15 May 1938.* Dublin, 1940, 480–9.

O'Neill. Joseph. *The Wind from the North.* London, 1935.

Opren, G.H. *Ireland under the Normans.* Oxford, 1920.

Otway-Ruthven, A.J. *A History of Medieval Ireland.* London, 1968.

Pentland, Marjorie. *A Bonnie Fechter: The Life of Ishbel Marjoribanks, Marchioness of Aberdeen.* London, 1952.

Perrin, Robert. *Jewels.* London, 1977.

Phillips,Thomas. *MSS Report on the Fortifications in Ireland (1685).* mss, National Library of Ireland.

Rocque, John. *An Exact Survey of the City and Suburbs of Dublin* (map), 1756.

Ronan, Myles V. 'The Ancient Chapel Royal, Dublin Castle,' *Irish Ecclesiastical Record*, 21 (1923), 353–370.

Roundell, Julia Anne Elizabeth, 'From a Diary at Dublin Castle during the Phoenix Park Trial,' *The Nineteenth Century and After*, LX, 1906, 559–575.

Rud, Mogens. *The Bayeux Tapestry and the Battle of Hastings 1066.* Copenhagen, 1988.

Rych, Barnaby. *A New Description of Ireland.* London, 1610.

Ryan, John. 'Pre-Norman Dublin,' *JRSAI*, 79 (1949), 64–83.

—— Review of George Little's *Dublin before the Vikings: An Adventure in Discovery. Studies*, 47 (1958), 206–208.

Sadleir, Thomas Ulick. 'The Romance of Dublin Castle. Personalities and Pomp in the Famous Citadel of British Rule,' *The Voice of Ireland*, ed. William G. Fitzgerald. Dublin and London, 1924, 57–61.

Shaw, Henry. *The Dublin Pictorial Guide and Directory.* Dublin, 1850.

Skinner, Liam C. *Politicians by Accident.* Dublin, 1946.

Slevin, Gerard. 'The Norman Irish,' *Ireland of the Welcomes*, 18, 1, May-June 1969, 40–42.

Somerville-Large, Peter. *Dublin: The Fair City.* London, 1996.

Speede, John. *The Theatre of the Empire of Great Britaine* (map). London, 1611.

Stanihurst, Richard. 'Description of Dublin 1577,' in *Holinshed's Irish Chronicle, 1577.* Dublin, 1979.

Stephan, Enno. *Spies in Ireland*. London, 1963.

Strangways, Leonard R. *The Walls of Dublin from All Available Authorities* (map). Dublin, 1904.

Thomas, Avril. *The Walled Towns of Ireland*, Vol. 2, 29–93. Blackrock, 1992.

Thom's Official Directory of Great Britain and Ireland, together with the Post Office Official Directory of Dublin and Suburbs. Dublin, 1844–1960.

Todd, J.H. (ed and trans). *Cogadh Gaedhel re Gallaibh: the Wars of the Gaedhil with the Gaill, or the Invasions of Ireland by the Danes and other Norsemen; The Original Irish Text*. London, 1867.

Tynan, Katharine. *Twenty-Five Years*. London, 1913.

Tryckare, Tre. *The Vikings*. New York, 1966.

Tuckman, Barbara W. *A Distant Mirror: The Calamitous 14th Century*. New York, 1978.

Victoria RI. *The Letters of Queen Victoria, vol. III, 1854–1861*, ed. A.C. Benson and Lord Esher. London, 1908.

Warburton, John, James Whitelaw and Robert Walsh. *History of the City of Dublin*. London, 1818.

Wallace, P. F. 'Recent Discoveries at Wood Quay', *Bull. GSIHS*, 5, 23–6, 1978.

—— 'The Origins of Dublin' in Scott, B.G. ed *Studies on Early Ireland*, Belfast, 1982.129–34.

Walsh, Peter. *Dublin c.840–c.1450: The Years of Medieval Growth* (map). Friends of Medieval Dublin and Ordnance Survey, 1977.

Ware, Sir James. *Annals of Ireland*. Dublin, 1705.

Ware, Robert. *A Description of the Castle of Dublin* [1675]. Gilbert Collection (MS 75), Dublin.

White, John Manchip. 'Tristan and Isolt,' in Glyn Daniel (ed.), *Myth or Legend?* London, 1954.

Woodham-Smith, Cecil. *The Great Hunger: Ireland 1845–9*. London, 1962.

Wright, Arnold. *Disturbed Dublin: The Story of the Great Strike 1913–14*. London, 1914.

Wright, G.N. *Dublin: An Historical Guide*. Dublin, 1925; 1980.

Young, Susan M. *et al.* 'Medieval Britain and Ireland in 1986,' *Medieval Archaeology* 31, 1987, 177–8.

Ziegler, Philip. *The Black Death*. London, 1969.

MAPS

Clarke, Howard B. *Dublin c840–c1450: the medieval town in the modern city*. Map prepared for the Friends of Medieval Dublin and the Ordnance Survey of Ireland, 1978.

Rocque, John. *An Exact Survey of the City and Suburbs of Dublin*, 1756.

Speede, John. *The Theatre of the Empire of Great Britaine*. London, 1611.

Strangways, Leonard R. *The Walls of Dublin from all available authorities*. Dublin. 1904.

Walsh, Peter. *Dublin c840–c1450: the years of medieval growth*. Friends of Medieval Dublin and Ordnance Survey, 1977.

SOURCES OF EDITED EXTRACTS

(The dates are those of the original publication.)

The Normans Take Dublin in 1170
Giraldus Cambrensis, 'Of the storming of Dublin A.D. 1170,' from *Expugnatio Hibernica,* in *Works,* ed. Brewer & Dimock. Rolls Series. (London, 1861-1877)

The Escape of Red Hugh O'Donnell in 1591
Beatha Aodha Ruaidh Uí Dhomhnaill. Transcribed from the Book of Lughaidh ó Clérigh with introduction and notes by Rev. Paul Walsh. Dublin: Irish Texts Society, 1948, pp.11-21.

A visit to the Castle in 1640
Sir William Brereton, *Travels in the United provinces, England, Scotland and Ireland,* ed. Edward Hawkins (London, 1844)

An Evening at the Castle in 1710
Joseph Sheridan Le Fanu, *The Cock and Anchor, Being a Chronicle of Old Dublin* (1845)

The Castle in 1798
George Little, ed. 'The Diary of Richard Farrell, Barrister-at-law (1798),' *The Capuchin Annual* (1944)

An Encounter with Major Sirr in 1837
Katharine Tynan, *Twenty-Five Years* (1913)

What the Queen thought in 1849
The Letters of Queen Victoria, ed. A.C. Benson and Lord Esher, vol. iii, 1854-1861 (1908)

A Castle Ball in 1882
George Moore, *A Drama in Muslin* (1886) and *Parnell and His Island* (1887)

Daisy Fingal's First Levée in 1884
Elizabeth, Countess of Fingal, *Seventy Years Young* (1937)

The Theft of the Crown Jewels in 1907
Thomas Ulick Sadleir, 'The Romance of Dublin Castle,' in *The Voice of Ireland,* ed. William G. Fitzgerald (1924)

One of the last Levées in 1913
Eimar O'Duffy, *The Wasted Island* (1913)

A Revolutionary at Dublin Castle 1913
James Larkin, address at Dublin Castle, from the *Report of Board of Trade Inquiry into the Dublin Strike,* chaired by Sir George Askwith (1913)

Inside the Castle during Easter Week 1916
A V.A.D. Nurse, 'A Nurse in Dublin Castle,' *Blackwood's Magazine* (December 1916).

Collins Man in the Castle 1921
David Neligan, *A Spy in the Castle* (1968)

Lady Fingal Goes Back in 1936
Elizabeth, Countess of Fingal, *Seventy Years Young* (1937)

ACKNOWLEDGEMENTS

Thanks are due to Freddy O'Dwyer, Denis McCarthy, and several other members of the staff of the Heritage Service, the Office of Public Works, and the Castle Conference Centre, for their kind help over aspects of this book. Freddy O'Dwyer, the distinguished architectural historian, has in prepaation a full-scale treatment of the complicated architectural history of the Castle buildings (to be published shortly by the Office of Public Works), and Anne Robinson has prepared a PhD thesis on the 'History of Dublin Castle to 1684', also unpublished, while Denis McCarthy has published, through the Government Stationery Office, a colourful visitor's guide which gives a resumé of the history and sights. And once again, my thanks to the Irish Architectural Archive for their resources. I am also grateful to Deirdre Quinn and Teresa Whittington at the Central Catholic Library, and the staffs at the National Library, Trinity College Library, and Pembroke Public Library for their assistance.

Thanks are due to Tony Roche of the Photographic Section of the Office of Public Works for his help; to Gerald Lyne for help with materials from the Genealogical Office, to David MacLoughlin of the National Library; to Damien Maddock and Robert Allen. Uncredited items are from the author or private sources.